THE
FIRST
PARISH

THE
FIRST
PARISH

A PASTOR'S SURVIVAL MANUAL

J. KEITH COOK

THE WESTMINSTER PRESS
Philadelphia

Book Design by Alice Derr

First edition

Published by The Westminster Press℗
Philadelphia, Pennsylvania

PRINTED IN THE UNITED STATES OF AMERICA
9 8 7 6 5 4 3 2 1

Library of Congress Cataloging in Publication Data

Cook, J. Keith, 1935–
    The first parish.

    Includes bibliographical references and index.
    1. Pastoral theology.   I. Title.
BV4011.C644 1983   253   83-6940
ISBN 0-664-24442-4 (pbk.)

To my dad,
John E. Cook.
He's buried in Ord, Nebraska.
He taught me a great deal about loving,
and I love him more every year.

With thanks
for the special help of
Ruth Cook,
Wendy Larson,
and
Barbara Weitz

CONTENTS

AN INTRODUCTION

A famous British pastor, Frederick W. Robertson, began his ministry with a letter to a fellow first-timer, saying, "The prospect we have, as far as human eye can judge, is a stormy one, and predicts more controversy than edification." Feeling so unprepared for his profession, he said, "We enter it almost without chart or compass."[1] He died young.

Many of us start with Robertson's nervousness. No chart. No compass. We know a lot about the Pauline epistles, but very little about church trustees. We know how to handle H. R. Niebuhr, but we don't know how to handle A. B. Dick.

Those differences, and many others like them, can render a minister disillusioned—soon to try schoolteaching or selling insurance. The pastor's family can be undone.

In seminary or Bible college it's fun to talk about Dr. Downtown Church who waxes and wanes over a huge group of groomed people under the awe-inspiring carillons. You might even do some student intern work there. It feels comfortable, well-equipped, and challenging. You could handle it. You're sure of it. You picture yourself there.

Then, near the end of your senior year, the calls come—from small churches in small towns you didn't know existed. After a few years in one of those places you wonder if *you'll* ever be heard of.

This book is meant to help the minister survive for years of fruitful and personally fulfilling service in the pulpits and parishes of the church of Jesus Christ. I'm a pastor and have been for over twenty-two years.

It will not be my purpose so much to explain why problems occur as it is to suggest many ways to deal with problems. I hope to help pastors discover ways of "doing ministry" effectively enough to honor their ordination commitments and to be personally happy about their vocational lives.

There are many more ways of doing ministry than presented here. I offer several facets of one model—a model for ministry which for me has been successful and helpful. Not everything that works for me will work for everyone.

It is important to be aware that "gaming" or "role-playing" is inevitable. Everyone dons certain garments or effects a set of manners for certain relationships and certain tasks. I draw attention to this because some readers may feel I am gaming with people in several of the techniques described in this book. I don't want either you or me to be a con artist, but I do want us to be artists. I want us to practice the skillful art of ministry.

The shepherd image of ministry is woven throughout the fabric of Scripture and in the historical witness of the church. The scrapes and scraps of human flesh and toil are many. They need attention if the world is to reach the wholeness God intended for his creation. It is the work of shepherds to pay attention. To be with. To love. To truly care for the flock. Imagine baptism without touching. Imagine teaching or preaching without first "hearing with their ears." Imagine feeding without "suffering with their spirit." Imagine tending without loving and helping and healing. Jesus did all those things. The main model for ministry is Jesus himself. Most of what Jesus did was a model for what his colleagues in ministry could and should do. In John 13 he said to the embarrassed Peter as he washed Peter's feet, "I have given you an example." We can follow his many examples as we follow our mighty calling.

The job is immense. It can often be discouraging, but it can also be rewarding. We can feel lonely, but we are not alone. I hope this book offers some ways of assuring the reader that his or her vocation in Christian ministry can be fulfilling. It can be successful. The job can be done.

The terms "pastor" and "minister" are used interchangeably in this book and have here the same meaning. "Congregation" and "church" are also used interchangeably.

I'll write the way I talk. It shortens the distance.

1

GETTING READY TO GO TO THE PARISH

Pastors meet parishes in many different ways. There are two main methods for getting parish and pastor together. One is the call system, in which a congregation chooses the pastor it wants and then "calls" that pastor, praying that God concurs. The other is the appointment system. The denominational hierarchy assigns a pastor to a congregation, praying that God thought of the same idea. Within and between those two systems lie subtle variations. Be sure to visit with some trusted person in your denomination to learn how you can appropriately utilize its system. My purpose in this chapter is to provide guidance helpful especially to those using the call system, but others can benefit as well.

WRITING A DOSSIER/RÉSUMÉ

The dossier, or the résumé, is essential to most ministers who live under the call system. Your dossier has one job: to get your name on top of the pile of candidates being considered by a pastor-seeking committee. That is it. Foot in the door. No more. Don't overdo it. Your dossier must tell the truth. It must tell about you. But it has only one goal: to convince a committee it *needs* to talk to you.

So keep the dossier focused on its function. A buckshot dossier that tries to hit every possible job target spreads itself so thin that it will probably miss those congregations whose needs match your talents. Decide what kind of work you want to do (for example, pastor, Christian education, youth work) and draw attention to the abilities you have that make you suited for that *one* kind of work.

Of course, a pastor is said to be all things, especially in a small church. Consequently, if you mean to be a pastor, refer to your interests and abilities in the many things a pastor has to do.

Keep the dossier sounding as if you know how to be a pastor. For example, a committee from the typical congregation would probably rather know that you have a skill and interest in leading Bible-study groups and youth groups and enjoy calling on the elderly than that you spend as much time as possible translating from Greek.

It's called "knowing your audience." Figure out what congregations and their search committees want, and write for them.

Start with a short to-the-point paragraph about your general qualifications, if your denominational form will allow it. Next, list experience and accomplishments, starting with the most recent first. Intern and fieldwork experience should be included if it is recent. If job titles you've had do not tell what you did, clarify. Never puzzle the people you want to attract.

Move on, then, to paragraphs that briefly and clearly enlarge upon the introductory paragraph. Let these supporting paragraphs be specific and direct. Let them tell about you and what you have accomplished. Too many ministers' dossiers tell more about former churches than about the applicants. For example: "The church here is old and losing members to the suburbs. It got itself deep in debt . . ." It's more helpful to say: "While I led the youth group at Belden Church the group grew from four to thirty. Twenty of those youth attended worship services regularly." A committee will take notice and know that that was a result of your work.

That's being specific and direct about what you can do—without bragging and without spotlighting the church.

The dossier must be brief. "If he is too long on paper, he may be too long in the pulpit," the committee may think. Sloppy spelling and typing, as well as unclear sentences, earn a journey to the bottom of the pile. A photograph helps only if it reveals a warm personality.

List five or six character references, people who know your work, your talents, and your integrity. But be sure you ask them two questions before you put them on the list: "May I list you as a reference?" and "Will you have anything even remotely negative to say about me if you are contacted?" Pastor-seeking committees really want the apostle Paul for their next pastor. With that high standard in mind, they have the habit of forgetting all the good things they have heard about you when a reference suggests even one negative thing. You cannot afford the luxury of assuming that a friend will say only affirming things.

Make sure experienced colleagues read your dossier before you use it. Ask them to red-pencil anything that is unclear or needs to be improved in any way. Your dossier must not be allowed to work against you. Do it well!

How to Choose a Congregation

It is sometimes said of mate selection that if you choose the right spouse, there is nothing quite like it, and if you choose the wrong one—well, there is still nothing quite like it. Congregation selection is something like that. Make or break.

God has a lot to do with it. Yet we know that God is abundant in his allowances for freedom of choice. So prayer helps.

Finding a church that fits your needs, interests, and abilities will make a big difference in whether you will remain in the ministry, as well as in whether your congregation feels served or cynical about ministers and ministry.

Start by choosing a kind of ministry. Some ministers prefer to be on a larger church staff. They have specialized interests or abilities that can be used only in a larger church. Some graduates feel that the best route to becoming pastor of a large church is to do a stint in the "lesser" but learning roles of a larger church. A few people feel that their abilities are boxed in by narrowly defined job descriptions sometimes found in large-staff situations. They may want to experience the full spectrum of functions they feel they will experience in a small one-staff-person parish. For them it may seem like developing ministry from the bottom up. Learning all of it by having to do all of it.

Do not be afraid of congregations that will be very challenging. Macedonia still calls for pastors to do some difficult work. They may be the best opportunities for needed service and for your own learning. Don't go to hopeless exploiting situations, but do allow real challenge.

Before you visit with a pastor-seeking committee, do some preparation. A properly prepared committee will learn very little about you in the personal interview. They will have learned everything beforehand by their own investigation. If they are surprised by something in the interview, then they probably did not investigate you well enough beforehand. The interview is mostly to seek confirmation of the favorable feelings they have about you. You too need to prepare as thoroughly.

Some denominations maintain a file of up-to-date information on every congregation. Get it. Read it several times. Ask yourself several questions, including the following:

1. Have the previous ministers stayed long term or short term?
2. Why might that have been?
3. What does the file say about:
   a. The church's sense of mission?
   b. The church's desires for the future?
   c. What the church is looking for in a minister?

4. Do my abilities match what the church seems to be
    looking for?
5. What does the form fail to say?

Show the form to another pastor. Ask him or her to point out
anything you may have missed.

Phone any ministers or other persons whom you know who
may live close enough to the church to know anything about it.
Ask many questions. Ask who, outside the congregation,
knows the congregation best. Call that person. Find the name
of another minister in the same town, of the same or a sister
denomination. Contact area judicatory executives or officers.
From these sources find the answers to the following
questions:

1. What is the age range of the congregation and of its
    officers?
2. What is the nature of the relationship the congrega-
    tion usually has with its pastors? Are there limits to
    what the pastor can preach?
3. Why did the last pastor leave? (You may even want
    to phone him or her.)
4. What is the nature of the study and activity life of the
    congregation?
5. What image does the church have in the community
    and in its association or judicatory?
6. Do certain families or groups have a "lock" on the
    life of the church?
7. Does the church provide a house for the pastor? If so,
    are the officers good about maintenance of the
    house?
8. What are the intended salary terms? Are there
    usually appropriate annual increments?
9. What expectations does the church seem to have
    regarding the role of the pastor's spouse? Can he or
    she seek employment without criticism?

10. What opportunities and freedom does there seem to be for family and personal relaxation and entertainment?

11. What is the direction in ministry and mission the congregation wants to take and will accept?

12. Are there unresolved doctrinal or moral issues in the congregation, or any other serious divisions?

13. What type of community is served by the church?

14. Has the church any special financial problems?

15. How many of the major facets of the congregation's life are done in ways different from the ways you were taught? (If, for example, the church school uses a curriculum you consider to be a poor one, you may be inviting conflict.)

16. Does the church have potential, or is it bound to wither and die?

17. What is the size of the congregation? (A parish that can provide 175 to 200 people in worship can usually support a budget adequate for ministry.[2] One pastor should be able to serve a congregation of up to 400 to 500 members.)[3]

18. Is more than one congregation involved in the potential call? How well do they relate to each other? (Almost one in five ministers serves more than one church.)[4]

19. If the church situation is a tough one, what plans and support (financial, program, planning) does the area judicatory intend to provide?

And if I were considering a staff position in a large church, I would phone no fewer than four ministers of the same denomination in the same city or judicatory and ask how staff people seem to get along with the senior pastor. I would ask each person to name still another person I could phone for straight information. In addition to many of the above questions, I would want to know these things:

1. How supportive do the senior pastor and other staff members seem to be?
2. How secure does the tenure of the senior pastor seem to be?
3. Would the person I am talking to ever consider going on staff in that church?
4. Are there any special problems I should be aware of as I consider the position further?
5. Is the senior pastor a "firstborn"?[5]

Have good information on all issues. Remember, no surprises in the interview, only confirmations.

Now for the interview. It's serious now. Take your spouse. The decisions made will affect his or her life. The spouse's place to be during the interview is beside you. However, he or she should not volunteer many comments. Committees tend to be greatly turned off when they ask a candidate a question and the candidate's spouse answers. A skillful, thoughtful candidate may need to initiate adequate entry for the spouse to express concerns and ask questions, if the committee fails to do that. The candidate may turn to the spouse to ask, "Did I forget anything, honey?" or "What would you like to ask?" The spouse should certainly have his or her concerns addressed.

Dress correctly. Wear clothing that conveys authority and seriousness and invites confidence. A medium- or dark-blue suit is best for men, with a white or plain light-blue shirt and solid or simple striped tie (no clip-on ties), black shoes, and black socks, preferably knee-length. No sport outfit. Men should not wear a green suit, or a leisure suit of any color. The color green and leisure suits cause people to question one's seriousness and suspect one's integrity. Sounds picky? People are influenced by such things whether they are aware of it or not. For a woman candidate, a well-tailored, conservative blue or gray dress or skirted suit is best. A simple but soft scarf or a brooch adds a touch of femininity. Correct or incorrect

dress will make a difference.[6] There is more on clothing in
Chapter 2.

Now that you are in the town and in the parish area, keep all
senses working. Do people seem friendly and happy with one
another? Observe the distance between words and ways. For
example, I was once interviewed by a committee that
enthusiastically assured me they wanted to try new ideas and
methods. But somehow the words came out of stone faces.
The same people spoke adoringly of their redecorated parlor
area, where we sat for the interview. But it was gray, with bad
lighting and nearly useless furniture—not antique, just
out-of-date. It said, "Don't change me!" and "Children keep
out." I couldn't see how a lively ministry could be conducted
with people behind stone faces in a building painted with a bad
embalmer's brush. The committee's words and ways were not
together. It was an important sign.

Look for these other signs:[7]

1. Weeds around the church say, "We don't care."
2. Gray interiors and dark-brown tile floors say, "We
   don't expect much life around here."
3. Mimeotone paper for newsletters and reports say:
   "Let's get by as cheaply as we can. We're task-oriented, not people-oriented, so dull is O.K."
4. Leadership that is much older than general membership says, "We don't want new ideas . . . don't rock
   the boat."
5. A locked lounge says, "We don't really like
   kids."
6. "Members Only" signs on the parking lot say, "We're
   wary of newcomers."
7. A hard-to-find-from-the-front-door office says, "Our
   pastor (or staff) is only for the regulars here."
8. "Pastor Parking Only" says a former pastor played
   king and the congregation fails to express its anger
   about such arrogance.

In other words, see how sensitive the congregation seems to be to normal human dynamics. It may not be that bad signs are all bad. It may truly be that what they really need is leadership. Try to sense whether that is true and whether you're that leader. You may be the Moses they want and need to lead them out of captivity into new lands.

If you've done your homework but the committee hasn't, you may need to be in control of the situation. Control is important. Don't be overbearing, nor a bulldozer—that will backfire. Know exactly what the interview is to accomplish, what it must cover, where it must go, and subtly help it to get there. The candidate may have to be the one who must make certain that every question and every expectation is put on the table and looked at carefully.

Pastor-seeking committees come in all kinds. Many are made up of people valuable to the parish but not especially experienced in the personnel search process. Many a candidate has sat with a committee that doesn't seem to know who leads, what to ask, or what to say. Take the initiative. You don't want the interview time to go slowly and seem boring. That may give the members of the committee the impression that you are slow and boring.

Say something like: "I am glad we could get together. We need to learn as much as we can about each other. I'm sure you have some questions. We have a few, as well. Would you like to ask some questions?" If they fail to pick up the lead, go ahead with something like, "Let me share some things I have observed since coming here." State things that are positive and affirming. If that still fails to unleash discussion and inquiry, move on with your questions. If the committee still does not inquire adequately, proceed to offer information about your abilities and your interests. Help the members know the things about you that they need to know. For instance:

1. The nature of your personal commitment to Jesus Christ

2. The nature and quality of your relationships with people
3. The nature and quality of your personal and professional ethics
4. The things you feel you do best

Answer their questions honestly and without rambling. If you are hit with what is known as "the killer question"— "What do you consider your greatest weaknesses?"—respond with *positive* weaknesses. If you are impatient, say you have a hard time with sloppy work. If you are stubborn, say that when you know an idea is good, you tend to push it harder than many people would like. Vices often do have their virtuous side. Find the gold in your character "defects."

You will want to cover a lot of the ground suggested by the many questions listed earlier in this chapter. In addition, you may want to discuss these things:

1. A job description. If there is one, be sure to discuss all points in order to be clear about meanings. If there is none, don't fight it. Many corporations have learned that job descriptions can box people in and talent out. They often prefer to find a talented person, suggest the area of endeavor, and let tacit job description develop in the process of doing the job.
2. Lines of authority. To whom are the pastor and others responsible in the organizational structure of the church? Who makes final decisions about such things as program, finance, personnel problems, and the pastor's house?
3. What the last pastor did best. They will want more of those things. It may reveal what he or she did most poorly, as well (but don't ask it—don't seem to put him or her down). They will want less of those things.
4. What two or three things the congregation would want you to achieve in the first year.

Now, if possible, ask to meet with the main board of officers of the church. Repeat most key items discussed in the interview, to be sure that the officers with whom you would have to work have the same understandings as the committee. This step will help avoid conflict in the future.

Then, often, comes the candidating sermon. Again, be sure to wear clothing that creates confidence and displays an attitude of friendly seriousness.

Do not revamp the worship service. That would say, "O.K., folks, I'm going to change everything around here!"

The sermon might best be a simple, well-stated expression of your personal belief in Jesus Christ, what impact that has on your life and ministry, and what you want your ministry to accomplish.

Be sure that you do not leave this main interviewing/candidating experience without a complete understanding of terms. Consider at least the following eight things.

1. *Salary.* State your problem if what is offered seems inadequate.

2. *Housing.* If a house is provided, ask that the trustees plan at least one annual inspection to assure that it is adequately maintained and updated. Most small towns provide a house to ensure that a place to live is available. Many urban parishes provide a housing allowance instead. Be sure that the allowance is large enough to rent or purchase a house equal to at least the average residence of the committee members and officers with whom you are dealing.

3. *Study-leave provisions.* Commonly two full weeks a year plus a few hundred dollars a year are provided for costs related to legitimate continuing education. It shouldn't be for an extra fishing trip where you hope to do a "fair amount of reading." A large number of agreements provide that both time and funding provisions may be allowed to accumulate for up to six years to permit extended study. It is unfair to expect to collect these accumulations when you depart from the parish.

4. *Vacation and time off.* At least one day off a week. Two

to four weeks vacation a year, including the same number of Sundays. Not to be confused with study-leave time.

5. *Auto expenses*. Reimbursement for auto expenses can take a variety of forms: a stated amount of reimbursement per mile (this requires a well-kept log); a church-owned credit card so the church receives and pays legitimate charges; or, most common, a stated annual amount of reimbursement. Congregations often need to be helped to understand that this is not income for the pastor but a church administrative expense, like the telephone bill.

6. *Arrival time*. When will you begin work?

7. *Moving costs*. Congregations would reasonably be expected to cover your full costs of moving, including your transportation, food, and lodging costs en route to the parish. At the same time, they expect you to be reasonable. Don't expect them to pay to move your rock garden. It would not be worth the anger it would generate the first day you get to town.

8. *Pastor's discretionary fund*. This is a separate, small bank account funded annually by many congregations. It permits the pastor to pick up the lunch ticket for a business lunch when appropriate, or to pay fees at a conference. That sort of thing. One third of all pastors have such a fund. The average is $340. Such a fund is less common among evangelicals.[8]

You may think of other items important to you. Get them on the table, written down and initialed by the committee or board chairperson. Misunderstandings are too costly.

2

GETTING ON BOARD
WITH THE CONGREGATION

The dossier, we said, was supposed to start out so well that its readers couldn't help wanting to interview you. Now that you have accepted a call, you need to get on board with the congregation in a way that makes the people of the parish keep wanting you for a long, effective ministry.

Jesus' service of installation took place in the River Jordan under the wings of the Spirit and by the hand of his cousin John. Then he slipped away for a private period of wrestling with the ways of doing ministry. How would he get on board with people? Would he do the splashy, spectacular things? Or would he go the slower, surer way of doing the sharing, caring things? He thought out his style, image, and how he would carry out his ministry.

Don't hide for forty days. It worked for Jesus, but it wouldn't work for you. It wouldn't sit well with the congregation to learn that you were inaccessible the first ninth of your first year. Yet you do need to think out style, image, and ways of doing ministry so you and your congregation can survive each other and even grow together in ministry.

LEADERSHIP STYLE

You are called to be a leader. What kind will you be? What will be your style of leadership? Hitler was a leader. Gandhi was a leader. So was Al Capone. They had different styles.

Leadership is a key to accomplishing any important task with people. You will inevitably develop a style, a way or manner of leading (or failing to lead) people. So let's work on factors that make a difference.

Though some pastors lead by pronouncement (the "Herr Pastor" who gives marching orders to officers and other underlings), most ministers prefer a shared leadership style. Yet, even though lay people are now assuming larger responsibility in church life, most of them prefer that the pastor be *the* leader rather than *one* of the leaders.[9] They don't want a pastor who barks out orders, yet they want more of a "take charge" leader than many pastors want to be. Parishioners want a pastor who proposes, persuades, and points out the ways and means.

The best leaders have certain characteristics, certain things that they do.[10] Among the most important are the following:

1. The best leaders have peer skills. They naturally treat co-workers as equals.
2. They know how to uncomplicate things for the people who have to carry through.
3. They have the ability to enlighten and explain and mediate in ways that ease conflict and moderate disturbances.
4. They have an uncanny ability to know what people want to know and need to know, how to extract and validate the appropriate information, how to build the delivery network, and how to disseminate the information effectively.
5. They can cope with unstructured decision-making. They are not undone by the unexpected. The counselee who walks in without an appointment does not destroy the temperament or the schedule. Studies show that the ability of a pastor to be flexible and versatile is both a virtue and a necessity for survival.[11]

6. They understand resource allocation. They know how to use time well.
7. They have entrepreneurial skills—the ability to take reasonable risks and implement innovations. They initiate action.
8. They can see issues and define them. President Lyndon Johnson once said, "Get your head above the grass."[12] Good leaders clarify and educate.
9. They are hopeful. While recognizing imperfection, the best leaders retain a sense of optimism. A study of schoolteachers demonstrated that when they held high expectations for their students there was an increase of twenty-five points in students' I.Q. scores. The best leaders are optimistic. They do not demand that people follow them, but they expect that they will.
10. They listen to people and respond to felt needs.
11. They do a lot of what they do best. They understand their own limitations as well as their abilities. They capitalize on their abilities.
12. They are consistent. They do not confuse people by being, for example, authoritarian in the pulpit, then permissive in counseling, then dictatorial at officers' meetings, and then friendly in social encounters.

That's a lot for a pastor to be if he or she is to develop a helpful leadership style. Yet every bit of it is important to the practice of ministry.

Your leadership style needs to give labor its due. Put in a day's work every workday. No parish has too little work to do—only work you may not want to do or can't see to do. You can get paid while being lazy, but the people who pay you will resent it. Parishioners who have to be at work at 8 A.M. don't understand why they still catch you on the phone at home at 10 A.M.

Give attention to detail. Leaders know that many gains are

won by honoring small, seemingly unimportant details. One pastor earned the ire of his congregation by not bothering to open mail or give adequate notice for meetings. Bad leadership style. Care given to so-called trifles aids ministry.

Learn to love and lead people where they are. Encourage them forward. Don't shame them forward. One minister commented: "My congregation wouldn't talk or sit by any long-haired males. I really got after them for that. I don't put up with things like that." Questionable leadership style. That minister has lost two churches since I heard him say that.

Loving is most needed for leading. Most people will go a long way with a leader who they feel genuinely cares for them.

Think out your style. And bear in mind what Robert Townsend said: "As for the best leaders, the people do not notice their existence. The next best, the people honor and praise. The next, the people fear; and the next, the people hate. . . ." When the best leader's work is done, the people say, "We did it ourselves."[13]

Roles

"More than one beleaguered minister has undoubtedly felt that the congregation calls him when they want the key to the restroom and the bishop calls him when he wants the key to the treasure house, while he is under the illusion that he has the keys to the kingdom."[14] So what's a minister to do?

"I have become all things to all men, that I might by all means save some." Those words of Paul (I Cor. 9:22) are a model for a ministry that works its way by means of many roles. The pastor is called on to be a generalist in an age of specialization. He or she moves from one role to the other, often without a moment's notice. The effective leader is, we've said, flexible and versatile.

There is no way of escaping the role expectations that congregations have or the role self-images that pastors have. Problems may arise when the minister discovers that he or she and the congregation differ on what a minister should be and do. The congregation expects one thing, the minister expects another.

For one thing, ministers, like most professionals, tend to think in terms of the specialized functions of the profession (preaching, counseling, etc.). Lay people usually think in more relational terms. They don't think "educator" or "theologian." They describe the minister's work in personal and pastoral terms: "He gets along with people so well." "She preaches such helpful sermons."

When lay people have thought in terms of specific roles, their thoughts have, for several generations now, remained the same: preaching, visitation, and counseling.[15] Most ministers want a broader spectrum than that. Or they want to switch to some specific role they prefer, such as community organizer.

Allowing for variations in the description of all roles and types, note that two types of role groups seem to be characteristic of minister types. There are the sect types and the church types. The sect type of pastor tends to be oriented around a charismatic ministry. He or she has a "total work concept"—is always available at all hours for all meetings and services. This type of pastor needs to be needed. He or she may want to administer any kind of personal problem a parishioner might have. And there is usually a strong emphasis on being a soul saver.

The church type of pastor is more oriented around a sacramental concept of ministry. He or she may have generally acknowledged work hours. While this type of pastor is available at other hours, within limits, all-hour access is not encouraged. This pastor does not try to solve all the problems and needs of parishioners. He or she would do more counseling and advising than actual conducting of administrative detail in parishioners' lives. A difficulty occurs in that many denominational and judicatory leaders want pastors to be church types, while parishioners of even nonsectarian churches often like ministers who are sect types.

For effectiveness and survival, pastor and people need to agree on role expectations. Otherwise they may become locked into serious no-win relationships. Let's look at several roles.

The *preacher* is a proclaimer of insight and information intended to persuade and change people in certain ways. The role of preacher is appreciated by almost all lay people and many ministers, but rarely by those who have left the ministry.[16] Preaching can be the main thing you do. Ernest Fremont Tittle, the great Methodist preacher, saw himself as primarily a preacher. Often, when people came to see him he would not leave his private study and interrupt his sermon preparation to see them.[17] That wouldn't work for most of us.

The role of *prophet* is a dangerous one. When the apostle Paul was being a prophet, he kept his bags packed. Prophets do not predict things. They stand before the people of God and announce, at great risk, "Thus saith the Lord!" Many former pastors saw themselves as prophets.[18] Prophets speak to the social ills they see, and work to bring about a return to social policies and practices that seem more in keeping with God's will. Every pastor must sometimes be prophetic. When the role is performed with great care and thoughtfulness it is a powerful, purposeful role. But prepare for resistance. And take care lest you confuse activism with thoughtful, prophetic ministry.

A *priest* is a conductor of ritual. A priest, by whatever title he or she is called, does not concede much authority. He or she may see himself or herself as a channel—perhaps *the* channel—for God's grace. He or she conducts services—baptisms, Communion services. Even a home or hospital visitation may be largely ritual, devoid of warmth and easy exchange. That's a pretty bleak picture. It need not be all negative. The human animal requires *some* ritual. Witness the handshake! Every pastor performs some of the priestly functions. Yet if he or she is primarily priestly, people may feel bored. They really want a pastor who can conduct ritual well when it is appropriate, but beyond that they want someone who gives more. It is not enough to "love a little, agree a lot, and make no waves."[19]

There is the role of *teacher,* one of the traditional roles for clergypersons. It is one of the major ways we equip people to conduct ministry in the world. The role of teacher requires a great deal of commitment, patience, and excitement about the learners as well as the content. One of the best pastoral things a minister can do is teach at least one Bible-study class each week. It will help the pastor, the people, and the parish in many ways.

Pastor is also a role. The pastor is the care giver, the feeder of the flock, the spiritual overseer. The role of pastor includes leading, problem-solving, counseling, and visitation. The pastor is tough when necessary, but also friendly and compassionate. The pastor proclaims the truth, believes it, and lives by it to the best of his or her ability. Pastors do shepherding things.

There is the role of *administrator* or *manager.* Some ministers despise this role. For them it seems to involve temporal trivia that gets in the way of kingdom-coming. Others enjoy it. It can give them the appearance of being busier than an auctioneer at a farm sale, keeping them safely insulated from doing "people things." You cannot avoid the role, or at least you do so at great risk. Good administration is essential; it greatly facilitates parish life and programming.

The role of *organizer* is not quite the same as that of administrator. It has less to do with management detail (letters, budget, records, etc.). It has more to do with goal-setting, development of concepts and the program activities that make up congregational life.

There is the role of *community model.* It is sometimes a heavy burden to be highly visible and at the same time to have to be a living, walking model of good morals, virtuous habits, perfect marriage, and exemplary parenthood. It is, however, the third most common role in which lay people cast their ministers.[20] People find it easier to follow someone of whom they can be proud. They want their minister to be a Christian example the community can readily respect. It's not a bad thing to be; it's a bad thing to *have* to be.

There is the role of *bellboy*. The bellboy pastor likes to be a "go-fer," busying himself or herself with being the congregation's purchasing agent, putting tables up (and, later, away), being supervisor for all repair and building projects, and doing custodial work. The bellboy may enjoy the role as an avoidance device—to keep from doing ministry.

Every effective minister performs all these roles at one time or another. Difficulty arises when a minister becomes totally committed to only one of the roles, or excludes any of the roles, or emphasizes certain ones while the congregation prefers others.

An appropriate balance must be achieved. Your interests and abilities should be very much a part of the consideration—as must be the understandings, hopes, and needs of the parish. The sorting-out process should begin when you are interviewed by the pastor-seeking committee and when you first meet with the officers. It should continue, allowing for modification, throughout your tenure.

If the previous minister was very priestly, the congregation may expect more of the same; or it may need more of a care giver, a lover, a pastor. It is important, however, to be sure that the roles emphasized and altered are done so in a shared way. Officers and key group leaders, at the very least, need to be aware of what is happening and to concur in the decisions made about them. Finally, remain flexible.

AUTHORITY

An interesting thing happened to me on the way to the gallows. I nearly fell into the trap. It was in my first parish. A woman in the congregation spoke to me privately during a time of difficult decision-making in the church. She said, "Just remember that you are the President of this place!" It sounded good. I even liked the capital "P" her pursed lips put on the word "President."

She was reared in another denominational system in which the minister was "the authority" in all matters. Therefore her words sounded good even to her own ears. Even so, another thing was happening. She was angling for her own position of authority. Those who confer titles sometimes have more authority and power than those who wear the titles. This woman wanted to tell me what was right and what was wrong, and I could preside. She was truly a friend, but we were in a contest for authority. It was a long time before I knew that. She may never have known it.

Authority and power work together. Jesus spoke with authority. It was very powerful. His authoritative stance brought crowds, miracles, change, and hope. His was creative and thoughtful use of authority.

In churches, as in many institutions, the people elect a leader. Sometimes, then, they retain the authority for themselves and delegate responsibility for execution to their chosen leader. When the leader wants to have the authority and delegate the responsibility, a struggle ensues.

Congregations often need to retain some authority, through their various governing boards and groups. Otherwise the variety of pastors they have through the years could exercise unbearable strain on the life of the organization. They may not want their pastor to decide to sell church property, to finalize the church budget, or to unilaterally decide at what hours the congregation will gather for weekly worship services.

At the same time, the pastor needs to have areas of authority. Frequently they include the content of sermons and prayers. Those are powerful areas in which to have authority.

There are three basic ways in which a leader gains authority: tradition, constitutional/legal, and charisma.[21]

Tradition has given the pastor a kind of aura of authority

that he may not be able to escape. It goes with the office. Some of us encourage it. We may appoint ourselves and our surroundings for it: the black robe, the high, massive pulpit, even the big expensive car driven by some pastors serving people of modest income levels. We may insist on certain traditional titles. We may have the Bible in hand for a portrait.

We have already referred to the authority many pastors have that allows them to decide the content of sermons and prayers. Often this is granted on legal, constitutional grounds within the denominational structure. There may be other constitutionally given areas of authority for pastors in certain denominations, or in certain congregational bylaws. They may be for a wide variety of things, such as hymn selection, deciding who is ready for confirmation, or what Bible-study course should be used.

Perhaps the greatest authority occurs when the leader has charisma—when he or she has a certain way with people, a charm, a magic, an appeal that arouses special popular enthusiasm for what the leader proposes and for where the leader may lead.

The way you are with people makes a big difference. If you remain accountable to the proper board or to the appropriate people, you will gain authority. If you genuinely respect the authority of the women's group, the women will recognize your authority and trust you with more of it. If you are a person who truly cares about the needs and feelings of elderly people and young people, those people will trust your projects and proposals. If you use authority to extend love rather than to dominate or rebuke or moralize, your words will carry weight.

Authority is assisted when it is used with reservation. People who spill out quantities of truth and opinion in answer to questions not asked tend to weaken their authority. Another disease that can erode authority is the inclination to rule on every subject. There have been pastors who want to decide what kind of dishes the church kitchen should have and what brand of organ the organist should play. Professional people who use authority most successfully use it only in those areas where they have demonstrated competence or are otherwise called to do so.

Part of the problem of authority is also how you feel about yourself. I was afraid when I realized that I, at age twenty-five, was now in a position to conduct meetings and provide leadership for a board of officers whose average age was fully thirty years my senior. They were skilled business leaders and respected farmers. I felt like a kid. I quickly found that when I confessed my mistakes, made clearly stated proposals with objectives they would appreciate, never insisted on my way, listened to feelings (even when not verbalized), and carried out their decisions well, they recognized my role. I became one of them—one having authority.

In our ministry we make and influence decisions—in a mutual process with parishioners—that seriously affect the lives of many people for years to come.

IMAGE

Images affect us significantly. The image we have of ourselves may burden us or empower us. The image others have of us also plays tunes to which we dance.

Our own self-image tends to be self-fulfilling. We sometimes have self-image problems that are related to personality and other personal factors, but some of the problems have to do with the profession. Many of us experience times of identity crisis. We're not always sure ministers are needed in the mainstreams of life. We see other people who seem more necessary. We may notice, if we serve in a small community, that people trust the local physician for counseling about family problems more than they do the minister. It can be hard on the ego.

Ministry is in an ambiguous position. The human community's value systems are in a state of flux. That causes strain for any community, and certainly for the people who are traditionally called upon to define, monitor, and sustain community values. In such a period of transition the pastor can at one and the same time be a pest and the victim of castigation if he or she does not uphold certain values. Couple that with the frustration a pastor may feel while observing that the average lay member wishes to maintain only a nominal commitment to the church, and a minister can feel very low on the totem pole.

It is realistic to understand that the minister's profession remains, in fact, critically essential to many people. Lives are indeed changed by the work we do in God's name. No other profession assembles so many people to sit voluntarily at its feet on a regular basis to hear what it has to say. Forty-two percent of all people turn first to their minister when they experience emotional stress. This exceeds, by a considerable amount, the proportion who would turn to any other source.[22] A psychiatric social worker showed me the results of some testing she had done with several of her counselees. Exactly half these counselees had listed their ministers when asked to name three persons they admired most.[23] We do help people. We need not think better of ourselves than is warranted, but we need to know that ours is a very important calling. Laugh with the crowd when it witnesses a clumsy, irrelevant minister in a movie. When we do our job well, our parishioners know that the screen caricature is unlike their pastor.

The so-called "third sex syndrome" image afflicts some ministers. We are called to conduct caring functions. Those are sometimes labeled "feminine functions." This can be a problem for male ministers. Earnest proclamation of forceful points of view from public podiums is sometimes assumed to be a masculine thing to do. That poses problems for female ministers. Those are not reasonable sex-role assignments. All the functions of ministry require both gentleness and strength. The quality of work will in the end determine what people think, unless, of course, your mannerisms are quite different from those common to the community or congregation. Just be yourself, as you would expect anyone to be. Don't let someone else's problem with sexuality be your problem.

Then there is the problem of looking like a minister. It's somehow a good feeling to hear someone say, "You don't look like a minister." There are, of course, ministers who nourish the image of the dowdy, humble-pie, and generally out-of-it image some people have of us. They do it for several reasons. Some just are that way; they're being themselves. Others might prefer to look sharper, but don't know how to go about it. They should seek the advice of a minister friend whose image they admire and trust. Others must think that "gray," "impoverished," and "out-of-date" is what is expected of them. They may fear that they won't get a fair raise if they wear a well-fitted suit. They choose to be the token poverty person—the parson in rags. Such thinking is a self-imposed imprisonment that misunderstands the sophistication of most parishioners, who would prefer to be proud of us rather than embarrassed about the way we appear. "Cadillac clergy" in a "VW congregation" would create a counterproductive image, of course. And so might the reverse.

John T. Molloy, the nation's most prominent men's clothing consultant, says that "60 percent of the people hurt themselves by their manner of dress" and that "we must dress to be credible." He noted: "John Kennedy dressed right. He used clothing as a weapon." In his list of ten commandments for dressing for credibility, the first two are (1) Wear subtle shades and (2) Wear beige coats—if you have one coat, let it be beige. He goes on to say that black and dark-blue suits with plain white or light-blue shirts and unflashy ties and plain dark socks and shoes are the most credible for persuasion.[24] Proper fit is important too.

Remain flexible, of course. When I went to my first parish, which was in a small town with many farm families, I could quickly see that suit and tie were out of place if I was going to

38   THE FIRST PARISH

establish a relationship of trust with most of my parishioners. And sloppy, grubby clothing would have worn badly with the many people there who understood the dynamics of proper attire. Facial hair would have turned away almost everybody. So I wore well-pressed slacks and open-collared sport shirts during the week for almost all purposes other than worship services. It was accepted. After about three years, when the congregation had learned to accept me for what I was, I could begin to dress up more, which was to my liking. Thoughtful attire can help eliminate barriers.

Sometimes we suffer from a sense of professional inferiority. "Many pastors have a . . . frightened view of their significance as pastors, and this seriously limits their effectiveness."[25] When the physician walks into the hospital room, one feels that the physician expects the minister to move out. As does the patient. It helped me when an older and wiser minister reminded me that we represent the Great Physician and that we are very much a part of the healing team even if the physician doesn't know it. We don't have to bully the physician. We simply need to know we belong. We carry on the ministry of Jesus Christ—without which people cannot well get along.

We may say that lay people can do much of what we do as well as we do. That is true, but we forget that for many people the minister makes a difference. No matter how much we may encourage lay ministry, the fact remains that, without the ministry of the clergy, lay ministry would not long survive. Parishioners look to pastors.

The use of profanity and so-called dirty jokes is an image item. Profanity and the telling of questionable stories needs to be practiced with great caution. It is inhuman to expect that they will never be used. Mark Twain said that swearing sometimes provides a comfort denied even to prayer. There is good humor regarding all the honorable facets of life, even the sexual. But there is a time and a place for everything. Four-letter words destroy too much credibility with too many people with whom we must deal. Jokes and stories with sexual overtones told outside close, understanding friendships will be misunderstood and destructive. They are not needed to make us appear to be "free."

Then there is the image called the "messiah complex." We take on that image when we insist on our way, when we know better, when we insist on our titles and our last names, and when we become the answer man. People know the difference. Even adults play the old childhood game called "King of the Mountain." They'll bring you down. Your pastorate will be short, or if long, ignored. When I was a twenty-seven-year-old pastor, feeling very professional, it helped me to have a woman pass me on the street and respond to my "Hello" with a "Hello, boy." She'll never know how that reached me. Many of us need that woman and her ministry to us.

Somewhat related to the messiah complex is the need some of us feel to be perfect. Jesus did say, "You . . . must be perfect" (Matt. 5:48). We misunderstand, however, if we think we must never expose any error in our own judgment, or any weakness or emotion. The gospel calls for maturity more than actual perfection. It is mature to admit mistakes and inabilities. Indeed, we set ourselves up for losing when we aim for perfection. We can't deliver. Ulcers are in the offing. Or heartache. We actually help our people when we allow them to see our faults and failures, especially when they can see, too, how we accept them and deal with them from a faith perspective.

It is also important for each of us to make a realistic assessment of the things we do well and the things we do badly. We can't avoid all things we do badly. If we don't feel adept at performing weddings but there is no other pastor in the church, then we do the weddings. But generally speaking, we should capitalize on our assets—by doing mostly what we do best. That's merely using one's talents to best advantage for the church, and for our own sense of worth.

Another factor of image and style is that of authenticity and integrity. Ministers must be what they say they are if anyone is going to listen and follow. People recognize phoniness. They spot defensiveness, or discrepancy between what the pastor says and does. People can see when something doesn't look right. There may be a professional facade that covers the truth or actual feelings. It makes the person sound like a robot who knows the right words to spew out.

Parishioners also notice when their pastor is being himself or herself. There is no doubt. He or she is neither defensive nor phony. The pastor is completely honest in his or her reactions.

People want those pastors. The most important thing they want in a minister is genuine commitment and personal integrity—a person who keeps commitments and carries out promises.[26] Many a minister has undone good work by failing to pay bills in small-town stores or to return borrowed tools, or by identifying with the poker-playing, bottle-tipping crowd. One minister tended bar occasionally in the small town where he was pastor. The parishioners saw him as a phony. They were done with him. To them he was not authentic.

People want a minister whose integrity includes a willingness to serve without regard for acclaim, who is not self-serving. They don't want ministers who avoid intimacy, who don't have time for people, who are critical, who deal with people with demeaning and insensitive attitudes. They understand integrity.

Finally, there is the "lover" image—in the best sense of the word. It is crucial. Congregations of varying types and denominations say that if a minister can't be good at all things, his or her weaknesses can best be overlooked if the minister loves the people. They prefer that much more than the next important preferences.[27] People really need to feel accepted and loved, warts and all. In I Cor. 12:4 to 13:3, Paul is pointing to love as the high gift essential to every form of ministry. "For whether a man preach, teach, conduct the affairs of the

Church, or engage in any other pastoral activity, if he has not love his ministry is nothing."[28]

There can be problems with the "lover" image. If it is feigned, it will fail. If it is a device for receiving gifts and attention, it will wear itself thin. If it hungers for acceptance, causing you to say yes to every demand of your time and talent, it will wear you out. If it evolves into anything even bordering on adultery, it may cost you your profession and your family, and the ugliness of it will drive some wonderful people away from the church for the rest of their lives.

Love is risky. But risk it. It was the central facet in the operational style of Jesus' ministry.

RELATIONSHIPS

The success of our ministry will probably depend most on the quality of our personal and pastoral relationships with the people we serve—assuming, of course, that the relationship we have with Jesus Christ is firm and growing. The New Testament church spoke of two levels of verbal communication, *kerygma* (proclamation) and *didache* (the ethical teaching). But a third and deeper level of communication weaves its way through the fabric of the written witness. It was there, alive and powerful. It was nonverbal. It was known in the *person* of Jesus Christ. It continues to be known to this day as the most powerful agent for the Christian cause—through people who are able to manifest it on a feeling level. It is the work of the Holy Spirit as it expresses itself in caring, sharing, living relationships. That is how healing takes place. And redemption.

Jesus worked in very personal ways. He was an outstanding personality. The best way to send an idea is to wrap it up in a person. That's incarnational theology. Our own personality is a critical factor in whether we can remain in ministry. If you are not especially congenial and not a "person person," you may need to work on it. Changes can be made, and need to be.

The most serious criticism people make of their ministers has to do with the minister being cold and self-serving.[29] The warmth of the personality of the minister is essential.

The caring personality is an open one. The few words "Let the children come to me" (Matt. 19:14a) consume so little space in Scripture, but they represent so much of the ministry of Jesus. His openness to everyone helps so many people see themselves and what they could become. Jesus was accessible. His simple openness made him the target of some people who wanted to manipulate him to their own ends. But he took those risks. He reached deeply into the lives of people, because he remained personally and spiritually available to them. Our ways with people need to demonstrate a willingness to engage them on their terms and to meet their felt needs.

We need to recognize people. It's amazing how easily good relationships are built and sustained by little forms of attention and recognition. A short stop to say "Hello, how are you?" when you meet a member on the street makes people feel attended to. The best conversations are fed by questions about the other person, rather than by offering information about yourself. A little wave of the hand and a smile across the crowded theater at intermission makes the member feel recognized. The feel is what's important.

Smile when you're talking on the telephone. Take a clue from the training plan of a large insurance company. New agents are asked to choose several names at random from the telephone book and call all those persons to make an appointment. With half the calls, the agent never smiles; on the other half, he or she *does* smile. All factors, other than the smile, are the same, but the success rate on the smiling calls is remarkably higher. Even on the phone, where it is unseen, the smile makes a difference!

Some ministers send a simple card to all members on such occasions as birthdays or wedding anniversaries. Some make a point of writing a personal letter of appreciation to one member a week. Find ways of saying thanks for almost any effort, whether it was folding bulletins or oiling the church furnace. Say it in person, mention it in a "These People Did Things" column in the church newsletter, or jot a note on a postcard.

Recognize the businesses in which your members are involved. One minister I know purchased three new suits one afternoon in a nearby town. That same evening he conducted the annual congregational meeting, at which he brashly told about his purchases that day. Many members felt angry about paying a minister "too much" if he can buy three new suits at one shot, something they felt they couldn't afford. But, worse still, at that meeting was an active member who owned and operated a menswear store in the community. It was the last time that merchant went to that church. People need to experience the validation of their life's work by their pastor, if it can be done. It's a very important contact. It's a way of caring.

Another important form of recognition is the use of names. Remember people's names and use them. Almost anyone who has the intelligence to get through college has the ability to remember the names of people he or she meets. I used to say, "I just can't remember names." Finally, I worked on it. I found that when I was introduced to someone, I rarely listened to that person's name. I was faking attention, but in fact mentally preparing for the next few paragraphs—designing the upcoming conversation. Therefore I lost the name. I began to listen hard to names, repeating them as soon as possible. ("Well, hello, Arlys McCorkindale. Arlys, have you lived here long?") I found that the conversation could usually take care of itself. During gaps in the conversation, or as I left that person, I would mentally repeat the name to myself. Or I found opportunities to introduce Arlys to other people so I could reuse the name, for reinforcement. Then I'd use her name the next time we met. She'd feel accepted and special.

Relationship-building requires a lot of listening and

pulse-feeling. Any minister who doesn't know what's going on with the members of the congregation is in trouble. We are called, in part, to love people with our ears.

Listening may be the most difficult of all human arts. It is truly an art, a very personal skill. Listening is so important that corporate executives say they spend at least 40 percent of their time listening.[30] Listening comes before preaching in the same way and for the same reasons that the examination comes before prescription and treatment in the case of a physician. We need to do more "finding out" than "speaking out."

Listening starts with the willingness to put forth the effort it requires. Ministers are called and paid to talk. We love it. Talking controls the conversation so it will remain safe and comfortable. It becomes difficult, then, to close the lips and open the ears. We may need loving spouses and friends who tell us to "shut up and listen." We may need to assign ourselves the project of listening, over and over again until it evolves into a more natural style. One of the simple and effective ways to listen is to spend our quota of words on asking questions and then let the other person respond. "What's your work?" "How much family do you have?" (Those two questions touch on the favorite things many people like to talk about.) "How is your mother after her surgery?" (Ask about things you know are important to people.) Then let them talk. They will think you are a wonderful conversationalist. And you'll find out many significant feelings and facts about those people.

Listen between the lines. Often the most important messages are in the words left unsaid. They lie in the face or the stance of the speaker. The handshake of a parishioner after worship might communicate, nonverbally, the message that something is different about this person today. She's happier than usual, or the grip is less generous than usual. It's O.K. to ask, "Say, what's making you so happy today?" Or to phone her later to say: "Forgive me if I'm wrong, but I felt that something was burdening you today. Is there any way I can be of help?" In other words, be alert to the normal mood levels of your parishioners. You will sometimes read the level wrong. You will sometimes run up against denials. But you will often find yourself listening to some very important moments in the lives of people. Even when those people choose not to disclose, they will feel you care about them.

Listen for ideas. Good listeners focus on central ideas. They appreciate and utilize the chitchat necessary to warm up most conversations, but they can tell the difference between chaff and kernel. Then they creatively and kindly move in on the kernel.

Listen for mood. Pastoral service begins with responding in the same mood. Respond appropriately to the pains and joy of others. Obviously no one chuckles when a person says his or her son just died. But there are less obvious moments when we are called on to catch the mood the speaker is experiencing and to respond to it. It is part of good listening and good caring.

Listen with your body language. When Adlai E. Stevenson talked to you, his eyes stayed on you. You knew that, as busy and important as he was, at the moment you were the center of the world for him. Do not succumb to distractions. Maintain eye contact. Forget your wristwatch. Don't complete peoples' sentences for them. Don't seize the subject and take over.

Resist sounding impatient. Don't expect your partner in conversation to be as organized in his or her thoughts as you feel you are. An authoritarian insists on his or her form, conclusions, or manner. It won't work. People need to say it their way. Enjoy the differences.

There are various mechanical ways of "listening" that help take the pulse of the parish.[31] Questionnaires, for example, are common, convenient, and often helpful. They provide security for the respondents, who can indicate some things they might not otherwise say. They have uniformity in that they ask everyone in the group the same questions in exactly the same way. Be aware of some pitfalls, however. Don't overdo the length or frequency of questionnaires or the congregation will tire of them. Ensure anonymity. Tell the respondents why the information is being sought and how it will be used. (One minister needed to reassure his congregation that a form evaluating his work was only to help him seek out areas where he could improve.)

Questionnaires should start with careful definition of what we really want to know. Then the right questions need to be asked to get the information needed. Many questions leave confusion about their meaning. The responses, then, are useless because they answer questions people *thought* you asked instead of what you actually meant to ask. Or the forms ask for information too difficult to deliver, ensuring minimal response. I read a church newsletter that included a form asking two questions for people to answer and return. One was, "Name three hymns that are your favorites," but the form provided space for only two hymn titles. The other question was, "What passages of Scripture would you like to hear sermons about?" Clear. Concise. A good idea. But people will probably ignore it because too few people can list passages of Scripture. It would have worked better to ask people to list Bible ideas and stories, or any other topics on which they would like to hear sermons. In addition, few people will take time to fill out and return forms from newsletters. Readers have their attention diverted as soon as the page is turned. A separate letter on only one subject with a return envelope enclosed is better. It is even better to have the form in the worship bulletin. Ask people to respond and hand it in then and there.

One of the most important pulse-feeling devices involves seeking out a couple of trusted, knowledgeable members of the parish. Buy them lunch or coffee and simply ask the questions you need to ask. "How are people feeling about the church budget?" "Is my preaching meeting the needs of people?" "What are the main compliments and main criticisms you hear about my work?" "What changes do you think I need to work on?" Ask your spouse too. He or she can be a sturdy source of loving, helpful criticism.

Finally, make inquiries of the people whose worship attendance habits change. If someone who never came suddenly shows up for four Sundays in a row, check that out. If someone who has been a regular misses four Sundays in a row, check that out too. Something important is happening, and you need to know. Ask.

There are a few more matters that assist in building and maintaining relationships in a parish. Teach something regularly, whether it is a Bible class or a night adult course, at least once a week. It will put you in touch with the parish people. People need it, love it, and are reassured to know you are indeed teaching Bible.

We'll all survive longer and serve better in our parishes if we can resist complaining about the church—either our particular congregation or the denomination. Nearly all congregations are as good as they know how to be until a good leader leads them to be better. There are faults, to be sure. We sometimes think the church is insignificant, feeble, and frustrating. Yet, by contrast, fewer than a third of the one hundred largest American corporations of fifty years ago exist today.[32] The church is lasting. It is still Christ's body, doing powerful work.

Here is another ingredient vital to any relationship: Ask for forgiveness when you make a mistake. Admit the error to the person or group involved. Apologize. Do it simply, quickly, honestly.

Finally, I repeat the most important factor in staying on board with the congregation: Be a loving, caring person. It seems ordinary. But it is so necessary—and so often missing. I once heard a merchant say to his clerks, "We all need to spend less time thinking about improving what we say to the customers and more time thinking about improving our attitudes about customers." It applies to us too.

SETTING UP FOR BUSINESS

You've been given a key to the church. The desk is clean. You're the only person in the building. Where to begin? As in *The Music Man,* "You gotta know the territory." "Territory" for ministry has more to do with people than with places. Yet the places where people and parish are are also important. You might start there.

Start from the desk out. Snoop through your desk and the files. Find out what the leftover letters talk about. Spend a good part of a day opening every cupboard in the building. Discover what resources lie in dusty, dark corners. Find out if the projector works. Get to know the building so you know where things are when you need them.

Now move out into the neighborhood. Get a mind's-eye picture of the parish. My first pastorate consisted of congregations in two small towns. I drew a street map of each community. Then I drew in every house on every street. Then I took the maps to an old-timer in each town and said, "Help me name every family in every house." We did the same for every place of business. I starred the homes and businesses of "our" families. I did the same for the farmhouses. Those maps were helpful in many ways, many times.

Another good first-day thing to do is to telephone some church officer to find out who is most in need of pastoral attention right away. Call on those people quickly.

Then get together with a group of persons who head the various organizations in the church—for example, the presidents of boards and the choir director. Ask them about meeting patterns. Let a calendar take shape for you. Ask these leaders what is needed most by the various groups and how you can best help meet those needs.

Over the next several months you will be making the most important contracts you will make with that congregation. They will be implicit and built primarily around expecta-tions—yours and theirs. So listen hard to expectations. Voice them to see if you understand. Clarify. Suggest alterations that can recognize the need and yet allow you to live without frustration. Meet with key leaders every few months to see if you are still on track with each other.

Consider the climate also. One of the most important jobs of executives is to create climate—climate in which good things can happen. Give careful consideration to the climate your office creates. If offices could speak, some would shout: "Don't come in! I'm not for people. I'm for ideas only." Others would say: "Welcome! Sit down. Let's talk."

Nearly all pastors have their offices in the church building. A few have their offices in a commercial building. (Main Street in a small community is a very accessible place to be. Keep the coffeepot going.) A few have their offices in their homes. The home office, for some parishioners, is awkward and lacks privacy. Try to have the office some place other than in your home.

Give thought to the way the top of your desk looks. Cluttered desks say to some people, "See how busy and important I am." But people won't believe the message. Maybe you'll be more secure than that.

Arrange your office so that you will not have to relate to visitors over a busy desk. Chairs around a coffee table in another part of your office offer much more of a person-to-person atmosphere. Select comfortable chairs. Hot coffee or tea says: "I'm glad you came. Stay a while."

Cozy surroundings remove the coldness that can get in the way of counseling and conferences. In your visits in the homes of parishioners, note the living rooms that have comfortable decor. Ask the people in those homes to help you achieve that same comfortable feel in your office. It will help create the right climate.

Spend some time thinking about the issues and methods facing you in the new parish. When I came to my second parish, I was struck by the comment of a member who said, "I like our church, but I'd never invite my friends to it." The congregation had a bad self-image. It became clear to me that one of my main tasks was to generate an improved self-image for the congregation. If the congregation could come to feel good about itself, many other important things could happen. It worked.

Many pastors in small parishes are startled to discover that they are also the church secretary—often with little or no equipment. If it happens to you, don't rebel. Parishes, like people, do the best they know how. Patiently and tactfully lead the parish to new understandings about providing adequately for the work to be done. Eventually volunteers can be enlisted to do secretarial work for a few hours a week. Build on that, but always without castigating the congregation. No new typewriter is worthwhile if it is given grudgingly by a groaning, guilt-infested group of donors.

3

GETTING THE JOB DONE

It would be impossible to cover all the facets of ministry, but here are several important ones.

ADMINISTRATION

The words "minister" and "administer" are similar. Both mean management, the providing of guidance so that important things can happen. A lot of ministers feel a frustration about administration. Some hate it. Some avoid it. Ministers say it is the task they value least. Yet they give an average of ten hours a week to that task—more time than to any other function except one.[33] Some ministers are anti-institutional. This affects their attitude toward administering the institution. But the machinery has to run.

We may begin to appreciate administration if we understand that it is nothing more than helping things to get done. Very few things in life can be done without attention to detail and to the machinery for moving things along. It is never enough to say the congregation must get from point A to point B. Someone has to find out how to get from A to B and then guide the steps. That's administration. That's the job of an executive. Ministers are executives. Christian education requires a lot of attention to detail. Feeding the poor requires good administration.

Inadequate attention to administration can erode the motivation many people in the church may once have had. I've known many ministers whose congregations became discouraged and demoralized by all the complications created when the ministers failed to do even the most elementary administrative things. Like opening mail! Letters were not answered. Important meetings were missed. Checks and bills to the church were lost. Hymns were not selected in time for choir practice. Little things, you say? But there comes a time when little things like that accumulate and cause a conflict. Careful administration is simply a courtesy.

Good management begins with planning. It searches out the needs, sets goals, establishes priorities, and defines the steps to be taken. Plan. Set a course. Know the route. Tend to details.

Organizing is next. Organization is the way the executive brings the group's resources to bear on the plan in order to achieve significant results. Suppose the plan is to have a new-member class. Maybe the appropriate committee should help decide what is to be accomplished in the classes. The dates have to be set, and the time of day. Who will be invited? Who will get out invitations? Who will teach what? Will there be a meal for the new members? Who will line up a meal? And on it goes to conclusion and evaluation. Organize. Careful attention to detail will help the plan work well and reduce the anxiety of participants.

People have to be motivated to use any plan. There may be recruiting, training, encouragement to sustain commitment. These are essential parts of the administrator's task. And you must have the right persons in the right spots. If you don't know who they are, ask. Selection of talent is the number-one ingredient in good management. Once you've put jobs in the hands of specific persons, leave those persons free to do their work. Offer whatever help and support they want, but don't do their jobs for them. Don't lead all the study groups. Don't be the program for every circle meeting. Delegate and develop leadership so the church can go on after you leave it. The delegation of work and authority is in itself a significant part of management. "Delegation takes place only if the superior's power has been transferred to the subordinate."[34] It must be a *real* transfer of power. More on that shortly.

We must also note that administering can become a crutch. Even for ministers who hate it, it can comfortably confine them to their desks if they let it. It can let them avoid the visitation they need to do. Administration gets in the way of ministry if you choose to complain about it—if you fail to discover that it oils the machinery of caring. If you think of letter writing as administration, it may be a chore. If you think of it as a way of caring, it becomes great ministry. Administration is a way of doing ministry. It is the art of weaving together needs, skills, hopes, schedules, and all kinds of resources to accomplish good things. It builds houses on rock instead of on sand.

TIME MANAGEMENT

More ministers are frustrated by the problems of schedule than anything else.

You will never get everything done. The only people who do get everything done are those who basically don't do much. They're like the teenager who can't see that the wastebaskets are full and begging to be emptied. I have yet to see a parish where there isn't enough work to keep a committed pastor busier than time will allow. The first rule is: Do all that time will allow, and refuse to feel guilty about what can't get done.

The second rule is: Work. We happen to be in a profession where we can get away with doing very little and still get paid. We can cover by saying, "I usually study at home till noon." Even when the congregation begins to feel that we really mean "from 11 A.M. to 12 noon" and that the main reading was the morning newspaper, people will let it go a long time before they cause trouble.

Some congregations get the feeling they are providing a lifetime scholarship for their pastor to do his or her "thing." It may be writing plays or working on another degree. Some of us dearly love to study. Much of it can be questioned as to whether it provides real support for the work of the paying parish. It may be a rip-off. One pastor I know raises hogs on the side. That's O.K. if it's actually done on free time, but his congregation began to discover that when he had to miss meetings at the church because he "had to be out of town" he was often in some neighboring town at a hog auction. Rip-off! Do the work the people pay you to do. That was the deal when you agreed to be their pastor. Raise hogs or be a minister. Decide.

Many parishioners can't understand why you and I can be home long after they've gone to work at 8 A.M. They don't like noticing that their pastor usually manages to take his or her children to school and pick them up when they, because of their jobs, have had to make other arrangements for their children. Get up and go to work. One thing common to most success stories is the alarm clock.

The third rule is: Don't complain about the work load you have. The average workweek for ministers is from fifty-three to sixty-seven hours.[35] Though the average full-time worker averages fifty-five hours a week, most farmers (who surround many of our smaller first parishes) average sixty hours, as do managers and self-employed business people.[36] So we're in the hour range of many of our parishioners. Our complaints will work against us.

If we are putting more than sixty hours into our workweek on a regular basis, then we have other problems. Even the most pivotal business executives are advised that if they are spending more than that at work, they are probably workaholics and are doing too many unnecessary things.[37]

The fourth rule is: Cut out the time wasters. There are many commonly recognized thieves of that precious commodity.[38] The worst wasters are listed first:

Time Waster No. 1—The telephone. The telephone can be a time-saver too. If you can confine the call to the subject at hand, an item of business can often be handled in less time by telephone than it would have taken to construct a clear letter. A quick telephone call to follow up on a patient consumes far less time than a hospital visit. The trouble is that telephones are so comfortable that a five-minute item can easily evolve into a half hour of chitchat. It is the role of the caller to close the conversation, but if he or she fails to do that, say: "I'd better let you get back to your work, and I need to also. Good to talk to you, Charlie." Access by phone is an item. Some calls (crises, for example) always warrant attention. My wife, children, key officers, and the secretary need to have access to me at any time. My children are aware of the need to begin with: "Dad, this can wait. Can you talk now or should I call back later?" (Unless, of course, it can't wait.)

If you are without a secretary and you see that the incoming telephone conversation could be dealt with at a less disruptive time, use some reasonable delaying tactics. Be fair, of course, but it is usually O.K. to say: "I'm involved just now. Can I look up some details and call you back at 4 P.M.?" Many good managers of time have regular call-back hours—usually in the last hour each morning and/or each afternoon. Both are times when most people are moving toward daily deadlines (meals and close of office) and are less likely to talk long.

Another valid and understood response is: "Say, Phil, I've got someone here just now. Can I call you back at 4:10 this afternoon?" Don't forget to call him when you said you would. Keep agreements.

If you have a secretary, he or she can help immensely. If I am not available, I've asked my secretary to say: "Yes, but he is with someone just now (or involved with something just now). Do you want me to interrupt him or can he call you back at 4:20 today?" She does not cut callers off. They make the decision, and interrupt only in emergencies. Many say they'll call back, or better yet, leave a simple message that takes care of it.

Time Waster No. 2—Drop-in visitors. We're in a people business. We may be busier than a candy store on Christmas Eve, but when a person in distress comes in, we quite appropriately behave as though we have plenty of time for him or her. Many managers deliberately design their day with one fifth of it for unexpected visitors.

Some drop-in visitors come too often. They enjoy a chat with "the boss." "The minister's got time," they think. Sometimes a creative secretary can head them off. It helps to have access to pastoral offices only through the secretarial office.

Some stay too long. These are the souls who try one's time. When Eleanor Roosevelt needed to have a visit conclude, she simply stood. One executive worked with slightly warmer attire and kept his office five degrees cooler than most people were used to. Shorter visits resulted. When people whom I really don't need to see come in—such as salespeople—I never sit down. I stand close to them, which encourages them to back up a little. I move in a bit. They back up a bit. I aim them toward the door. If we don't need what they have to sell, I quickly but kindly tell them. If a parishioner is staying too long, my secretary will arrange a phone call that demands my attention and helps conclude the visit. She may walk in to say, "There's someone here to see you, Keith." It may be her mother.

Sometimes nothing works.

Time Waster No. 3—Meetings. When meetings accomplish some purpose, they are important. They are a part of our lives. If you hate them, you can find another profession, or you can make them effective.

First rule: Don't attend every meeting just because it's called. "The pastor who programs himself for omnipresence is simply presumptuous. The Bible calls that 'sin.' "[39] Our advice or control is simply not needed for every committee to function. I rarely meet with the property committee. I feed the chairperson the items I notice need consideration. The members of the committee are competent to decide and act. At the same time, I never refuse to attend. No need to declare war. Our officers respect my day off each week and don't even suggest that I attend any meeting on that day.

Second rule: Never attend a meeting that you expect won't last as long as the time it took you to drive to it. In many rural areas you can drive four hours for a two-hour meeting. Don't.

Third rule: Help make the meeting move. I'm impressed with how long it takes many groups to make and second motions everybody already favors. If I'm chairing, I simply say, "Wally, will you move that?" and, "Jean, do you second that?" "Discussion? (Slight pause) Here's your chance! Going . . . going . . . gone. Those in favor . . ." Get on with it. If I'm not chairing, I often leap in to make the necessary motions and then poke the person next to me to get a second.

Help the discussion keep on track with: "This is important, but not quite on the issue. Can we deal with first issues first?" Ask the questions and make the statements that help a group clarify, reach conclusions, and make decisions.

One of the deadliest things groups can do is to spend a lot of time on dreary business. Most of the group could hardly care less. The women's organization in one church I know spent a full thirty minutes discussing what kind of can opener to buy for the kitchen. It was the last time some of the baby-sitter-paying younger women ever attended. So I say to the officers of groups: "Ask the full group to make only those decisions which absolutely require the full group—then cut that in half. Simply announce the decisions the board has made. If there is a serious problem with any of those decisions, there'll be a loud roar and changes can be made."

Our main board has a rule: The meeting will end in two hours. That board has several subcommittees, each of which is instructed never to ask the full board what to do about any issue. Rather, committees are to report their actions and to make recommendations for full board action. To do otherwise forces the full board to do the committees' work for the committees.

There is more on how to make meetings productive in the section on meetings, later in this chapter.

Time Waster No. 4—Lack of objectives, priorities, and deadlines. The best managers spend the last five minutes of a day previewing what they need to accomplish the next day. They spend the first five minutes of a day reviewing what they need to accomplish that day. They decide which must be done first, second, etc. Then they set out to do it. I work on things in reverse order of sequence. If I am to chair a meeting at noon, make a report to a committee at 3 P.M., and make a speech at 7:30 P.M., I work on the evening speech first, the afternoon report second, and prepare for the noon meeting last. That way I walk into the noon meeting with everything for it fresh on the edge of my mind. If I'm going to have to review my preparations for these events, I'd rather spend the review time on only the last two events than on all three.

Time Waster No. 5—Personal disorganization, indecision, and procrastination. Paperwork frustration is caused by indecision. A manager should be able to make an immediate decision on nearly every item in the "in" box. He or she probably won't know a bit more about the subject later. Why read a letter twice? Answer it now! If a short response is all that is required, I often jot my note right on the margin of the original letter, put it in an envelope, and send it off.

Time Waster No. 6—Attempting too much. Each of us has times when everything bunches up and there is too much to do. If that happens frequently, however, we've broken an important rule: No module of time should include more than one major responsibility. Morning, afternoon, and evening are each a module. Each module can accommodate minor duties in addition to a major one. But when you see that more than one major task has to fit into most or many modules, you've accepted too many responsibilities. The frenzy will be counterproductive. Trim. Adjust. Or suffer.

Delegation is necessary for the busy manager and minister. Some people can't distinguish between being busy and being productive. They may be working at the wrong things—things other people ought to be doing.

Except in emergencies, I do not shovel snow on the church walks—not because it is beneath me (it isn't), but because I know that if I begin to do such things, I can get stuck with them and the church members will be robbed of the handles they need to grip for the push and pull that makes the place theirs.

A minister whom I know and his wife do almost everything for the congregation. The church newsletter is replete with news about upcoming meetings, noting that "Pastor Cox and his wife will present the program (or lead the study)." That may be nice, but the pastor is playing daddy, and the congregation and its functioning committees and groups fail to mature. They've been hand-held.

Delegation requires a lot of sacrifice. Sometimes we'd rather do the work ourselves. Delegation requires a lot of trust because it gives away control, including quality control. But try it. Give away work, responsibility, and accountability to individuals, committees, and other groups.

The amount of control you continue to exert over a delegated responsibility should be limited to the *minimal* amount required to operate as an early warning system that permits remedial action to be taken on major problems. Good delegation helps groups and individuals mature for greater lay ministry and frees us for other leadership. Get a good book on delegation.

In delegating, as in all your work, strive for excellence but never for perfection. There is a difference. Excellence is attainable, gratifying, and healthy. Perfection is a waste of time, because it is unattainable, frustrating, and neurotic. The cost of perfection is prohibitive. Try for excellence.

Time Waster No. 7—The inability to say no. It's a disease. We feel guilty if we don't attempt to meet everybody's needs. But take a sensible look at the situation—at best we can't meet everybody's needs. How much less so if we dissipate our strength by responding to all requests?

It's important to evaluate work and do only the essential and desirable things. A minister I know has for years conducted a certain newcomer visitation program that has never resulted in a new member. When asked why he does it, he says, "Because I was asked to do that when I first came here." Evaluate. Decide what's worth it and what isn't. Say no to nonproductive work. Success may depend as much on what you don't do as on what you do.

I say no to all meetings on Mondays (my day off). I say "No, thank you" to nearly all wedding rehearsal dinners. "No" is not a four-letter word. It will save time and energy for better service in the Lord's name.

Time Waster No. 8—Fatigue. You get little done when your body and mind are dulled by fatigue and tension. These maladies stem from within the worker and not from without. Relax.

Four clues. Take your full vacation every year. You do no one a favor when you fail to take all your vacation. Get out of town, sit at home with your telephone off the hook—whatever.

Take a day off every week. Every week! Without fail. Any minister who is too busy to take a day off each week misunderstands his or her importance. It is manageable. Choose a day. Fasten it down. Announce it. Ask the congregation to help you keep it. Then *you* keep it. Yield only to funerals. Don't enter the office that day for any reason. God needed a day off. It is presumptuous of us to think we can get by without it.

Take a vacation every day. A ten-minute nap on the office carpet. A midmorning coffee break with the coffee shop gang or the office staff. I find it relaxing as well as relationship-building to walk through rooms where circles and other groups are meeting to chat with persons present—during their own coffee breaks, of course. I try not to disrupt their study or business.

And finally, work no more than thirteen modules each

week. I work all morning and all afternoon each Tuesday through Saturday. Ten modules. Two evenings. Twelve modules, now. Sunday morning. Thirteen modules. The rest is for my family and for me. I even arrange for all wedding rehearsals to be at 5 P.M. so I can have the evening free.

COMMUNICATIONS

People are usually down on what they're not up on. I keep that chiseled in my mind. Pastors and parishioners have to keep informed or they can surely get down on each other. Information has to pass both ways. Constantly.

Relationship is the goal. In the process, information will be exchanged. Persuasion will occur. Strategies for communication have been high on my agenda in each pastorate. Both the congregation and I have to be "in the know" if we are going to trust each other and work with each other. With good communication many battles can be settled before the first shot is fired.

Communication is essential and achievable in congregations of every size. Indeed, communication *will* occur in every congregation. The question is whether it is accidental and destructive or planned and constructive.

Good communication requires using the language of the people. You may have heard of the minister who said to his trustee committee, "We need a new chandelier in the parlor." The officers said: "No. None of our wives would know how to play one. What we really need is more light." Yes, more light. It requires you as the congregational officer in charge of communication to use their language. Don't use the big words you learned in school.

Communication includes inquiry. One good question is, "How do you feel about that?" Another, at appropriate times, is, "Did I injure your feelings?" Pay close attention to the feelings of every member of the church.

It is sometimes helpful to use more structured devices for

congregational pulse-feeling, temperature-taking, and infor-
mation-gathering. Sometimes I put a simple, clearly stated
questionnaire in the Sunday worship bulletin to find out what I
need to know. I've asked questions like:

> Do you wish I'd preach from the pulpit, or is it all right to
> preach from the open platform?
> Do you usually read ____ all of the newsletter?
>   ____ some of the newsletter?
>   ____ none of the newsletter?
> Do you have any sermon ideas you wish I'd use some
> Sunday?
> What part of the worship service do you appreciate most?
> What part of the worship service do you wish we'd change?

I've brought groups together to inquire and inform. One
such group is what I call my coffee-shop cabinet. I've had one
in each parish. None of its members have ever known it. It has
been simply a collection of trusted persons who, in my first
parish, happened to gather at a local coffee shop. Over coffee
I could ask, "How do people seem to feel about . . . ?" I
could also inform them of my ideas. "Would it work?"
Those sessions can be tremendously helpful two-way communication devices.

It's imperative to do the same thing, only more so, with the
church officers. Inquire and inform. Inquire and inform.
Continuously. And resist reacting to negative information
with hostility or defensiveness.

When my denomination takes an action that is potentially
explosive (for example, Angela Davis, ordination of homo-
sexuals), I waste no time informing the congregation in detail,
in person. First I telephone every denominational source
necessary in order to get all the facts. Then, on the very next
Sunday after the action, I explain every detail and share my
feelings as well as what I feel is a biblical position. It is
important communication that informs the congregational
family before the media start alarming them. In every case it

has defused people before any bombs go off. "People are usually down on what they're not up on." I could, of course, take an angry, fearful position myself and engineer their hostility toward the denomination. I resist doing that. We're in the resurrection business, not the crucifixion business. Inform and interpret positively.

Some devices are designed purely for information. Individual letters are useful. Notices on the hallway bulletin board are of questionable value: few people see bulletin boards. Information in the worship bulletin announcements reaches the active, attending portion of the congregation, but not all of the congregation.

Church newsletters can be the single most useful informational device you can use. I marvel at the effect our monthly newsletter has on the life of the church. Many ministers fail to appreciate its importance.

Indeed, the newsletter is wasted in some churches. It fails to inform. It provides an unprofessional, even sloppy image of the church. These are the rules I have for a good newsletter:

1. The pastor should edit the newsletter. As pastor I am in better touch with all of what's going on in the church than any other person. I am the main information officer of the congregation. I do not delegate the writing and editing of this important tool to anyone else. It is too important.

2. The newsletter should be used to inform people about what is *going* to happen far more than about what happened last month. It points toward the future rather than the past. One newsletter I receive often has little more than the word-for-word minutes of the circle meetings that occurred the previous month. Dead!

3. The newsletter is to have news, not cute nothings whispered into congregational ears. For example:

Ideas for Spring Planting
Plant five rows of peas: preparedness, promptness, perseverance, politeness, and prayer.

Next plant three rows of squash: squash gossip, squash criticism, squash indifference.

Then plant five rows of lettuce: let us be faithful, let us be loyal, let us be unselfish, let us love one another, let us be truthful.

No garden is complete without turnips: turn up for church, turn up with a smile, turn up with a new idea, turn up with real determination.

(Borrowed).

Junk! If I haven't enough material to fill a good newsletter with real news about what's happening in our congregation and in our denomination, then not enough is happening and I'd better do some creative program-planning! "Sweet nothing" poems and articles may please some people, but serious church workers will dismiss the newsletter as drivel and look for a better church.

4. The newsletter should not be used to scold a congregation. For instance, I'd edit out the following article which appeared in one newsletter. (I've changed the names.)

Education Orientation—
Everything but People!

It was a great program. Jane Jones had worked for days developing economical, worthwhile projects. Ron Weller gave an outstanding presentation on learning centers. Lori Miller explained the church school outreach program.

Only eight people showed up. Is that a measure of our interest in our children? Is that an indicator of our Christian commitment? Where were the over fifty workers and parents?

It is discouraging to those who expend effort when no one comes. . . .

It would have been better to visit privately with five or six key families to see why attendance was so low.

5. The newsletter must be easy to read quickly. I studied the *Kiplinger Washington Newsletter* and similar report pages in *Business Week* and elsewhere to see how they were designed to be read by busy executives. As a result I use black ink on excellent-quality yellow paper. No twill tone, which says, "We're trying to get by cheap. This communication isn't important." Articles have descriptive titles that stand out clearly on the left edge of the copy column so a reader can move quickly down the titles and select the articles he or she wants to read. I try to keep sentences short and pithy. The copy must be well typed and well printed. The newsletter must present no cumbersome barriers for readers. We staple down the left side so the newsletter opens magazine-style, so we can print on both sides. Lots of white space. No cute line drawings from those church newsletter service companies. They make the newsletter look like a grade-school paper.

6. The newsletter should never be used to thank the many people who give the minister gifts at Christmas. I don't want to appear to be encouraging more people to give me gifts next year. Anyone who gave me a gift deserves an individual thank-you note.

7. The newsletter should use lots of names. In spite of number 6, above, I will thank people for anything they did for the church. Anyone who fixed a screen or mowed the lawn, for example. I underline every member's name anytime it appears in the newsletter.

8. The newsletter should not be used as another chance to preach. It's difficult to keep "From the Pastor" columns from being preachy. The newsletter is for news.

Program and Goal-Setting

Someday you will ask yourself, "What am I doing here?" You've asked a good question. Don't let it pass as rhetorical. Answer. Figure it out.

Your church will have, at the least, worship services, and

probably a church school, a choir, something for youth, etc. Your church's program is important. Used well, it will accomplish significant things for God's people. To do that, you need to know what you want your programming to accomplish. That requires investigation, reflection, and setting of goals.

Pastors, like most executives, tend to focus on efforts rather than on results. The majority of executives say, "I manage the accounting department" or "I supervise seventy people." Few say, "I have to think through and prepare the material the officers need to make good decisions."

Planning is required for good results. Many congregations do little or no planning until a crisis occurs. That's not entirely bad, because few things can really happen until there is a felt need. However, a creative church will not *wait* for a crisis to do planning. When a new pastor arrives, a congregation is usually at the height of its expectation. Seize the ripe time for setting sights and establishing direction.

We want people to respond to our work. They are most responsive to leadership that is committed, positive, and problem-solving. Fence-straddling and foot-dragging simply serve to increase the anxiety of people. To avoid that anxiety, the leader has to understand and be committed to realistic, meaningful goals.

People are often confused by such terms as "goals," "objectives," "result objectives," and "performance objectives." Often it is easier just to say:

1. What we want to accomplish (the goal)
2. What we need to do to accomplish it
3. Who will do it
4. What resources are needed
5. What time span will be required
6. How we will check progress and know when we're done
7. Who will evaluate and how they will do it

The simpler the detail under each category the better.

The pastor is a key person in the whole process. You may be the main supplier of resources. When that is the case, take care to be helpful. One minister angered his "doers" by responding to their requests for resources by simply handing them piles of catalogs. They needed some of his mind and some helpful leads, but they felt they got none of that. So in anger they dropped the whole project. Be helpful. Look for signs of apathy, indifference, and lack of participation, which indicate an illness in the project. Maybe the goal was not broadly agreed upon as significant. Maybe you delegated authority to the right people, but demoralized them by, in effect, retaining control. The signs may say that somehow people feel contracts are not being lived up to.

It is essential that the whole goal-setting process be a mutual matter involving you, as the manager, and the congregation as partners. Unilaterally established goals are bound to provide pain and problem sooner or later. No project or program is meaningful unless there is a high level of motivation in common. Business executives say that the major reason projects go sour is that the real decision makers aren't in on the planning process. Bear in mind that in many congregations some of the real decision makers are not elected officers. They may sit quietly on the sidelines. They may or may not expect to be asked their opinions, but it is probably wise to pass most upcoming decisions before them. Their wisdom as to what will or will not work may be extraordinarily valuable to the success of important goals. In my first parish, the president of the local bank was a wonderful Christian man who never chose to impose his will on any church or community activity. But his commitment and wisdom were so trusted by the community that it really helped the elected leaders of the congregation to know that "Earl thought it would work." In some other congregations it would, of course, be better not to mention that such nonelected decision makers were in fact part of the process. The point is that all significant goals must be mutually arrived at and mutually owned.

Keep the goals you establish for yourself simple. One pastor says that for the first year in a parish he tries to accomplish four basic things:

1. Acceptance. Let the local uniqueness of the community emerge; every locale has some beauty, and your enjoyment of that will enhance your acceptability by the people of the parish.
2. Visibility. Lots of visitation.
3. Trust-building. Everything that needs to happen later depends on this base.
4. Self-education about the congregation and its ways.

Survival goals are usually self-defeating. Sometimes we become blinded to the fact that more people rally around the genuine proclamation of the Word than around the survival of institutions. When the work of the gospel is the center of our work, survival is nearly always an enjoyable by-product. Keep your mind on the right things. May our main goal be the increase among people of the love of God and neighbor. That keeps faith with what most congregations want. Usually the four most important issues faced by the congregations are:

1. Deepening the life of faith
2. Strengthening the youth program
3. Strengthening the church school
4. Raising the level of biblical knowledge among the members[40]

Remember, too, that congregations need victories. No army has the spirit to keep fighting if it has seen no victories. Congregations have to see and understand the progress made. They need to have ways of celebrating the steps forward. That's why mortgage-burning ceremonies are important. Such newsletter notices as "We've paid our mission pledge on time this month—for the first time ever . . . we're getting on track" help a group feel better about itself. It is important therefore to set achievable goals which can fulfill rather than frustrate the congregation. Mid-project thank-you letters from the pastor are rewarding. Even small satisfactions along the way make goals seem attainable.

An important question to ask is: "If our church were not already into this activity, would we get into it now?" If not, you may want to find gentle ways to get out of it and divert energies elsewhere. Remember that timing and gentleness are essential, because people do hate change, even when they say they want it.

There are four criteria common to congregations considered to be successful.[41] Successful congregations are *inclusional*—ready to employ all creative means to make the preaching of the Word and the sharing of the Sacraments available and clearly understood by all believers regardless of age, race, or class. Successful congregations are *affectional*—profoundly joyous and supportive of fellow members, exerting a conscious effort to lead the members to see each other and all humans as persons. A successful congregation has a *theological* concept of itself—knowing why it exists, that it is a community of disciples of Jesus Christ put in this time and place to do his work. Last, successful congregations are each *perpetual in hope*—they know God is and will be God forever, so that the secure future molds the present in peaceful ways which encourage members to go about their church work and their secular work as forms of ministry. Good items for our goal/direction setting.

In the process of planning program and setting goals, do these few things. Think future. Keep in mind where the ship is going. Do what I call "thinking twenty." Ask, "What will be the twenty-year effect of what we do now?" Question assumptions—yours and theirs.

Think wide. Recognize the multiple problems and multiple paths to the solution of problems. If you get locked in on your own one-way answers to problems as a way of opening up a congregation, you will *be* the problem rather than the solution. Pay attention to the functioning system. It is rarely as static or moribund as we assume. Use the dynamic forces present in existing systems whenever possible.

THE USE OF VOLUNTEERS

The second most common frustration in our work is dealing with volunteers. One of the most exciting things about the church is that it has accomplished so much through the volunteered effort and support of literally millions of people through the ages. These are people who love the Lord and are willing to give away large parts of their time, energy, and assets to do his work.

But let's face it, most people don't get up each day and put church work on the top of their priority list. Some people have the gall to put family first. Even jobs. Even golf.

Volunteers sometimes act as if they aren't being paid. We'll cope better when we accept the situation for what it is: The pastor lives in a world of volunteerism; many volunteers are not dependable; but many would die for the church and its most meaningful work.

Many people do give time away. The pastor, to use those bonuses, needs to know a few facts about volunteers. (1) People in the West, South, and Midwest are more generous in giving away time than easterners. (2) College-educated people give more time than lesser-educated people. (3) Older people give more time than younger people. (4) Nonwhites give more time than whites. (5) Women give more time than men. (6) Church people give much more time than nonchurch people (for all volunteerism, not just church work). (7) Evangelicals give more time than nonevangelicals.[42] We need to appreciate that even the most dedicated officer, with rare exceptions, considers the church to be the third priority in his or her life—after business and family.[43]

One way to improve the use of volunteers is to choose the right people for the right jobs.

In the selection process ask, "Who can do this job *especially well?*" When people are asked to do jobs they can't do well, they may wind up feeling embarrassed and overtasked out of the church. Ask people to do most what they do best. Resist asking people to do a job just to get them involved. It won't work, unless it truly is a task known to be of keen interest to the member.

Respect the preferences people have for arenas of work. Some people will do almost any job except that of standing before a group of people to speak. Respect their fear. Some parishioners will enjoy visiting people who are elderly and ill—they will do "people things." But some people prefer doing "thing things," such as typing. Appreciate and utilize those differences.

Maintain the motivating factors. Provide for satisfaction by providing (1) good working conditions, such as compatible companions for the task, favorable rules and regulations, clearly stated assignments, thoughtfully prepared facilities, coffee and cookies; (2) opportunities for recognition and enrichment, such as meaningful work and praise; and (3) growth opportunities. Probably the deepest motivational challenge is the chance to grow personally and spiritually.

People may not request thanks, but it needs to be given. Privately and publicly. Brief letters of gratitude are almost essential. Recognition encourages volunteers. Without it people begin to feel overworked and underloved—they burn out.

Resist any form of ridicule of those who never do anything. It happens that 73 percent of American Protestants (74 percent of Roman Catholics) don't give away time for any charitable work.[44] Refuse to be bothered by something you can't change.

Worship Services

The congregation celebrates its sense of community most fully when it worships. Worship is where some members make their only contact with the congregation. Worship will be where some members have their only exposure to the introduction of God's will, Word, and way into their lives. The worship service is very important.

Most pastors list the preparation and leading of worship as their third most important ministerial function.[45] However, congregational members and officers tend to feel that the first priority of the congregation is worship.[46] We do well to make major investment in the art of leading worship services that help people hear the Word, achieve a sense of community, and realize growth in commitment. When the services of worship do these things well, the congregation will grow. People will attend.

Here are some hints that may help. They work for me.

Work on the room. Atmosphere and surroundings have a huge impact on functions that occur in them. When I came to my current parish and needed to overcome the lack of the feeling of community, I worked on the worship room first. There was plenty of space, so fourteen feet had been allowed between the pulpit and the front row of chairs. Five feet was provided for each row of chairs. The center aisle was six feet wide. It made sense for comfort but was terrible for creating community. If we're going to get together for worship, let's really get together! The chairs were moved forward one inch each week so no one would notice (people hate change). The front row is now within four feet of the pulpit. The rows are now three feet apart, heel to heel. The aisle is four feet. It helped.

Lights should highlight the speakers when they are speaking. Cold colors hinder, warm room colors help. Careful attention to usher training assists in creating a setting for worship. Every detail in the room makes a difference.

Think about whether you should preach from the pulpit. In some situations it is best to preach from the pulpit. If the congregation would allow it, however, consider standing in front of the pulpit instead of behind it. In many ways President Nixon maintained distance, but in one way he eliminated a separating factor used by his predecessor. He got rid of the huge podium and battery of microphones Johnson always stood behind for press conferences. Nixon stood there simply, facing the folks, with a single microphone on an unobtrusive floor mike stand. Picture your teachers in school. Do you see them teaching from behind desks or right up front, close to the class? Picture Jesus. Do you see him communicating with people from behind a hunk of furniture with only his head showing? The pulpit can be very separating.

Try memorizing the Scripture so you can look the congregation in the eye as you share the Word. You might be amazed at how much better people listen. Don't panic if you forget. The people will stay relaxed if you do. When you forget the next verse just say, "Oops, I forgot." See what the next verse is and go on.

Not every word of a chapter has to be read in the Scripture lesson. Edit out verses that are not necessary to the flow of the idea for the morning's learning. John 11, for example, can be reduced by nearly half and still catch the story line necessary for many sermons. Some verses in some passages are very helpful in a Bible-study group, but encumber a worship service by leading people off track from the idea being highlighted for the day's sermon. Don't bore, confuse, or sidetrack your listeners. Eight to-the-point verses serve better than twenty-seven that lose people.

Choose hymns people enjoy singing. Every pastor has heard the words "I wish we could sing more of the old songs." That means, "I want to sing songs I grew up with." The hymns *everybody* grew up with can probably be numbered on half a hand. The only way to win is to have a few Sundays a year when no hymns are preselected and let the congregation call out the hymns they want to sing, right then and there. I rarely use more than two hymns in a service. That provides some singing for the singers who never joined the choir, but doesn't overdo it for the many people who hate hymn time. On Sundays when we have a "congregation calls it" hymn sing, we sing eight: four at first and four later, but only the first stanza of each. We're still not overdoing it, and yet several people have sung several of their favorite hymns.

On the other Sundays I try to choose hymns generally known and loved by the congregation. I learned long ago that to force a congregation to learn new hymns was for my satisfaction, not theirs. Of course, there are some wonderful new hymns that need to be tried. Of those, however, I consider only the ones I'm sure people would really learn easily and truly enjoy. And on the Sunday when I introduce an unfamiliar hymn, I make sure the other hymn used is very familiar and loved. Change comes hard for many people. They need some comforts.

Consider asking people to greet each other for a moment if they don't generally know each other. Small communities would find that phony. They already know each other. If you include that, however, just call it a greeting. "Passing the peace" is not part of real language for most people. Let people be natural.

Prayer is one of the most meaningful parts of worship for many people—especially if there are ways in which they can participate. I am continually amazed at how many worshipers feel deeply moved when, each Sunday, I ask if people have prayer requests. Several hand in pieces of paper. I read them out loud—my uncle is dying of cancer . . . we're grateful for our daughter who is ten today . . . help us with our marriage problem. They're much the same every week. But they are on the minds and hearts of these folks. Then we proceed to pray for those things. It is very personal and very meaningful. We don't ask worshipers to verbalize their requests. Several would be too shy. Written requests allow input from more people. It is a special time.

I've also found that people really respond best to simple, straightforward language in prayers and preaching. "Redound to thy glory" sounds odd to most of them. "May what we do please and honor you" says it for more people.

The celebration of the Sacraments can bring much to the lives of worshipers. But it must be meaningful. A caring church always celebrates the Sacraments in ways that are clearly understood by everyone. Use language that people use. Share what the Sacraments mean to you personally. Study the nuances of drama that can add to the real drama of those events. Not dew-covered roses for sprinkling a baby—that's melodrama. But careful delivery of words so that they don't sound read. Or thoughtful, unaffected handling of the elements. Breaking an actual loaf of bread is so much more real in its drama than pulling apart a cube of bread or cracking a wafer. Prescoring the bottom of the loaf with a knife takes away some of the drama. Good drama is pouring the juice or wine slowly from pitcher to chalice as all remain silent, listening to the tall thin stream fall. Use a glass pitcher and glass chalice. Let people see the wine or juice. Helpful drama. Don't be eager to reform a congregation by converting them from juice to wine. Either will do, so why start the war?

In baptism consider some personal approaches. People find them meaningful. Instead of having "Baptism Sunday" with the impersonal assembly-line row of parents with babies, try baptizing only one family's baby or babies at any one service. "When it's your day, it's your day." You'll have more baptism services, but they are significant for the Christian community. Take the baby in your arms. After the baptism, bring the lights up in the worship room and walk down the aisles with the baby—all the way back. Let the congregation see that baby. The parish will wrap its heart and love around that baby in a way never felt before. It helps seal the corporate contract just established in baptism. I talk about the history and meaning of baptism as I walk those aisles.

Finally, practice. I get to the church early to get my voice into shape. I rehearse the Scripture, trying each phrase in different ways until I find the way that best catches the meaning and flavor of the content. I ask myself, "I wonder how Paul would say this if he were just saying it instead of writing it?" Then I practice saying it that way. My job is not just to say words. My job is to convey meanings. Content must be prepared, and so must its delivery.

PREACHING

Any minister who underestimates the power of the pulpit is apt to miss the greatest opportunity he or she can have for significant ministry. Most Protestants attend worship services primarily to hear the sermon. We may say they should come to *worship,* but they in fact come mainly to hear helpful messages for their lives.[47] For many people, the sermon is the one moment in the week when they get in touch with God. People really do hunger for God's Word. They may not say it that way, but that's what keeps them coming. They hope to receive some word of guidance, comfort, inspiration, and support for another week of living the trials of life. How shall they hear without a preacher? Sermons change lives.

The church is in business to proclaim the Word of God, to set forth a road map for life. Our preaching must spring from the Word. Indeed, good preaching is speech by God through us rather than about God by us.

In his final charge to his chief of staff, Peter, Jesus said, "Feed my sheep." That's our job. Preaching is one of the ways we get food to the flock. They come expecting to be fed.

One of the first things to consider in our role as preacher is whether we will be prophetic, priestly, or pastoral. There will be times when we will be all three, but for the most part we choose one.

To be priestly may mean that the sermon is mere ritual—something to get through so we can get on with more sacramental functions. That may be appropriate in an altar-oriented denomination. It is not appropriate when it happens because we have relegated the sermon to a low level of importance or because we are failing to invest adequate time and energy in preparation. It is not true that a sermon is a sermon is a sermon. Sermons can move and shape the minds of people.

Priestly preaching tends to see as its role the upholding of tradition. Sometimes that's because certain traditions are valuable. Sometimes it's because it's easy and pleasing to the people who pay us. We must be careful about our motives when we preach in that way.

Prophetic preaching usually has much more power in it. And risk. Prophets are the "thus saith the Lord" proclaimers. They set sight on the problems in society, view those problems through the lens of the Word, and speak the message God means the world to hear concerning crucial issues. Where would we be without Amos and Martin Luther King and others? We are all called to speak out at times. Years ago our pulpits were used to bring God's judgment to bear upon child-labor practices. More recently, our preaching changed some minds on racial issues.

There are some cautions to consider. Jesus said, "Behold, I send you out as sheep in the midst of wolves." The wolves really show their teeth when prophets start to speak. Prophets tend to land hard on the status quo. People hate change. The clash comes quickly. Preachers who assume the prophetic stance and fail to realize that conflict is inevitable are in for more personal anguish than they may be able to bear.

When one spouse repeatedly pesters the other with the same or similar requests, it is called henpecking. Henpecking, or nagging, is usually counterproductive. Just so with some prophetic preaching. John Wesley said, "No man can be bullied into heaven."[48] Some of the preaching we call prophetic turns out to be bullying. It can do a congregation more harm than good. Some ministers made that mistake in the days of racial strife. Too many congregations felt they suffered a long parade of Sunday lectures pestering them on their sinful attitudes. Worshipers turned off their ears. Others fumed inside and opted out of worship attendance. Others asked their pastors to resign. We mustn't wear people out with our persistent wisdom.

Here is the way this minister worked it out. I feel called to speak the truth as I see it, based on God's Word as I understand it. I will do that on the significant issues of the day. I will say what I feel needs to be said even when I know I stand alone. However, I have the conviction that I must not too often get too far ahead of the congregation on issues or I will destroy my capacity to lead. A general who gets too far out in front of his troops may be mistaken for the enemy and take fire better saved for the real enemy. So here are Cook's Rules for Prophetic Preaching:

1. Speak on volatile issues while the problem is hot. Speak clearly and forcibly, but only once a year on any one issue.

2. Space prophetic sermons so that there are several pastoral types of sermons between each issue-oriented sermon.

3. Relate the issue to a biblical message and make the connection clear.

4. Help parishioners understand that these ideas are offered for their *consideration*. They are not required to believe what I believe. I make it clear that I know that I am not wiser than they are.

5. Never preach a sermon on a controversial issue without giving time in the service for at least a dozen people to rise—on their own volition—to have their say, pro or con. I take the first twelve who stand regardless of who they are and regardless of what they have to say. If any speaker cannot be heard by the entire audience, I repeat the comments over the public-address system so all can hear. And even if the

comments are severely critical of what I've just said, I ask the speaker whether, in repeating his or her comments, I've conveyed the message correctly. I do not argue back. It is unrealistic for a congregation to have to sit there and take what I've got to say on a hot issue without having an opportunity to express another point of view. This really lets off steam right then and there. After a dozen comments, almost everyone's feelings have been expressed. They feel better. They don't have to go home to have the proverbial roast preacher for lunch. They see me as fair-minded. It eases the way for acceptance of what I have to say.

6. Speak lovingly. "Radicals get into trouble not so much because they are radicals as because they are fools. . . . My own increasing conviction is that you can say anything that needs to be said to people whom you love and . . . know that you love them. . . . It is not necessary to be rude in order to be honest."[49]

The parishioners and I are equals dealing with some trying issue—attempting to bring God's Word to bear on the problems of our time.

Pastoral preaching attempts to care for the hurts and felt needs of people. It never seeks to preach to people where they should be; it seeks to preach to people where they are. It keeps a finger on the parish pulse—to discover not what would be easy for people but what would be healing.

When I want to find out which sermons seem to speak to people the most, I ask the congregation to list the two or three sermons they remember most. Inevitably they remember the sermons that deal with prayer, suffering, marriage, the Commandments, death, worry, forgiveness—the things of which everyday life is made. So I preach those things.

There are various kinds of sermons and preaching styles. Some work. Some don't.

Some sermons turn into lectures. A common style. It is generally appreciated by anyone whose expectation of the sermon is that it be informative but otherwise sterile A lecture is chiefly concerned about a subject to be elucidated. A sermon, on the other hand, is chiefly concerned about people and seeks to persuade them to move from one point to another, from one degree of commitment to another. Few who preach lectures know they do so. You can perhaps tell if you have slipped into the practice of lecturing if—

1. Your sermons deal more with subjects than with people. You may be preaching to answer questions no one is really asking.
2. Your sermon titles have no action in them. They begin to sound as exciting as "Why We Have Elders" or "The Nicene Creed."
3. You haven't asked (and answered) the question, "As a result of today's sermon, how do I want the hearers to feel and what do I want them to do?"
4. The sermons turn out to be monologues. No one engages you in a discussion, either during the hour or in the narthex at noon.

Dialogue sermons can be helpful if used sparingly and done naturally. All sermons done in forms other than what the congregation is accustomed to must have an important purpose and be done very well—and very seldom. I once did a sermon in first person. It worked well. People responded enthusiastically. So I did four more of them that year. I discovered that that was three or four too many. They wore thin rapidly. I learned that one a year was enough. Dialogue sermons seem like a natural when you have an associate or a capable lay person to debate or otherwise deal with a subject before the congregation. The trouble is that they rarely turn out to be natural. They die. They are often too canned— read-out-loud sermons from symmetrically placed lecterns. The only dialogue sermons I use now are the ones that happen without notice, when someone in the congregation is moved to raise a hand and take me on or to add thoughts to what I'm saying. It will happen occasionally if the parishioners discover that you are not rigid and are willing for the sermon to be a participatory event.

Sermons in the first person can be powerful—as long as I remain me even though speaking the message of the chosen character. For example, when I was Mary the mother of Jesus at Golgotha, I made no attempt to dress like Mary or to raise the pitch of my voice. I made no attempt to fool anyone. I was me. I made no attempt to be obviously dramatic. I simply used my normal postures and normal pace to say: "I'm Mary. Jesus was my son. I wish you could have been with me the day the hammers drove nails into my boy's hands and feet. It hurt me. Maybe you parents know something of how I felt . . ." The congregation saw and heard me, but they thought and felt Mary. To overdo it would embarrass people and distract from the message. Know the story so well you can do it without notes.

In the long run, the ordinary, when well done, is best. The traditional sermon, with its beginning, main points, and conclusion, is hard to improve upon. Doing it well is the key.

Here are a few things that have worked for me:

1. I keep the sermon short. Mark Twain said that it is a horrible death to be talked to death. A woman in my first parish used to say, "Any minister who can't say what he has to say in fifteen minutes hasn't got anything to say."

2. I let my personality show through. It adds life to the event. E. F. Tittle said, "Preaching is . . . the presentation of truth through personality."[50]

3. I can be personal, but I must be careful not to dwell on me and my family, not to brag. I can point to my joys and problems as representative of those that other people have.

4. Be biblical. Frederick Robertson always based his sermon on a Bible character in action. It was almost a miniature case study. He preferred to deal with a person who lived the truth rather than with an abstraction. I do that often. However you do it, people need to know without a doubt that what you are talking about is based on the Bible, and on what you genuinely believe.

5. I preach in the vernacular. *Reader's Digest* level of language. It is presumptuous and wasteful to do otherwise. Whoeverstartedthewordthatneverseemstoend, anyway? And why did we start using it? If I am to speak to people, I need to use their language. Plain. Ordinary. Everyday. When I find it necessary to use a word like "incarnation," I take time to say, "That means coming into flesh, God coming in the form of a man—Jesus." The moment you lose even one or two people with a word they don't understand, you may have lost them for the rest of the sermon. It isn't worth that. A plumber wrote to the Bureau of Standards saying that he had found hydrochloric acid good for cleaning out clogged drains. The bureau wrote back: "The efficacy of hydrochloric acid is indisputable but the corrosive residue is incompatible with metallic permanence." The plumber replied he was glad the bureau agreed with him. The bureau tried again, saying: "We cannot assume the responsibility for the production of toxic and noxious residue with hydrochloric acid, and suggest that you use an alternative procedure." The plumber wrote he was pleased that he and the bureau saw eye to eye. Finally the bureau sent a message that came through: "Don't use hydrochloric acid. It eats the hell out of the pipes."[51] Plain talk.

6. I use affection and humor. Both need to happen naturally—when I force them they fail. Listeners are better able to get hold of an idea when they can chuckle, and when they feel the message comes in love. See I Corinthians 13.

7. I make the sermon an oral event. A sermon written and then read to a congregation is more of a literary event than an oral one. In an oral event, the speaker keeps his or her eyes on the hearers. The speaker plays with the sounds of words and phrases as well as their meanings; the words are delivered to convey emotion as well as information. An oral event gets away from the manuscript in order to respond to what's happening between pastor and congregation. It has electricity. It is an event. Every Sunday a very large number of truly

oral sermons are delivered in this country, most of them by black preachers. We can learn something from them. An outstanding article on oral sermons is Keith Watkins, "Banishing the Disease of Literacy," *Worship* Vol. 47, No. 8 (October 1973), pp. 482-488.

8. I avoid waging campaigns, attacking other denominations and people. I avoid warlike vehemence and scolding. People are never scolded into shape. They are loved into shape.

In all of this it is important to know the audience. Only a fool would attempt to gain the attention of the thousands present at a Super Bowl game in order to preach to them. That would be a gross misunderstanding of the moment and the mind of the audience. It would test parishioners' patience to preach on homosexuality on Christmas Sunday, or on the feminist movement on Thanksgiving. Congregations know a lot about the right times and places for things. Congregations need Christmas sermons on Christmas Sunday. And when momentous events occur, they need to be addressed so people can deal with them from a Christian point of view. In her plea for guidance from the pulpit, Rachel Conrad Wahlberg wrote: "The Sunday after the Kent [campus] killings I heard a minister preach an Old Testament passage as if nothing had happened. My thoughts were screaming at him: Are you dead? Tell us how to respond as a Christian to this crime!"[52]

Power in the pulpit depends upon a profound understanding of and respect for the people in the pew. It is practiced in part by working as if you and the congregation were equals. Genesis 11 talks about a tower that caused confusion and separation. It still happens today. It happens when preachers play God to congregations. I know a preacher who stands in a vaulted, thronelike pulpit high above the heads of his congregation. He is tall, but even so he puts a box on the floor of his elevated pulpit so that he rises even higher over his upward-bent parishioners. He speaks eloquently, but his tower sends a message of its own. He obviously expects no one to differ with him. But they do—behind his back.

The practice of equality with the audience requires participation by the listeners. Participatory sermons begin where people are and allow give-and-take somewhere during the body of the sermon or afterward. We've already talked about allowing people to speak up. As for beginnings, grab the minds of people. Paul did that. He understood and reached his audiences by beginning where they were. In the synagogue in Antioch he cited the Old Testament they loved (Acts 13:26-41). In Athens, where no one knew anything about the Scriptures, he quoted their own Greek poets (Acts 17:22-31).

Begin in an interest-catching way. One sermon began: "Sin is not a popular subject, even in the church. Our attitude is much like that of the little boy who was standing on the chair with his hand in the cookie jar when his mother entered the kitchen. When asked what he was doing with his hand in the cookie jar, he replied simply, "I'd rather not talk about it!" Good story! But the first line could be livelier. Try this: "Did you hear the one about the little boy who was standing on a chair with his arm stretched into the cookie jar when his mother came into the kitchen? When she asked him, 'What are you doing?' he said, 'I'd rather not talk about it!' I get the feeling most of us would rather not talk about sin—the times our hands get caught in the company till, or when we've done anything else to harm relationships. We'd rather not talk about it because, like the little boy, we already feel convicted. But we *need* to talk about it." That gets attention better.

The content of the sermon has to be important and has to lead to something. It must not, for example, be designed to discuss repentance. It must be designed to persuade people to repent.

I've learned that my sermons need to include a great deal of biblical interpretation. Like it or not, that's all the Bible many good church folks are going to get. But Bible interpretation can be deadly if it is not presented in lively and interesting ways. The Bible *is* lively and interesting, but dull interpretation can do it in.

Use many illustrations. The worst ones come from books. The best ones come from your experience. When you want to use personal experiences that include anyone else in the community, be sure to get that person's permission, even though you may not disclose his or her identity in any way.

Quotations are boring. Listeners are more interested in what *you* think than in what your favorite authors think. Trying to follow a spoken quotation is more work than most listeners want. Avoid them.

When you first get into a parish you will be too new to preach its pulse. For those first several Sundays, why not simply share your own faith? "This is what I feel deeply about Jesus Christ . . . the Bible . . . God's creation." Therein lies a series of sermons that will help the congregation begin to know you. Such sermons can help the members know they can trust some of your basic theological concepts.

As for delivery, I remember well the day an officer in my first parish commented on how much my sermons seemed to improve when I switched from preaching from manuscript to preaching from notes. I remember the day several years later when, shaking under my robe, I left the security of the pulpit, stepped out in front of the congregation, and preached without notes. I've never preached from a pulpit since (except as a visiting preacher—some congregations would be put off by the strangeness of it on a one-shot occasion). This is not to say that everyone should leave the pulpit. It is only to say that we should experiment with various ways until we find the method of communicating that works best for us.

As for manuscript, one needs to remember that people hear conversational language better than they hear literary structures. Not many people can write like they talk. There is the benefit of precision in writing out the sermon, and following it closely at 11 A.M. on Sunday brings that precision to the congregation. But consider risking some loss of precision and even losing a point here and there by speaking with, or without, notes. By the time you have written a sermon, it will be enough a part of your being that you may be able to bring it from your mind. What you lose in dropping a few immortal phrases penned on paper you gain in developing a unique, free, participatory style of delivery.

Some ministers spend two or three days preparing a sermon. Others do it Abe Lincoln style—on the back of an envelope in an hour or so. Some prepare early in the week. Others, Saturday night. Anybody's way and timing is all right as long as the sermons serve the congregation well. I spend about three hours on a sermon—almost always on Saturday morning so it will be fresh in my mind Sunday.

As I begin to prepare I ask myself, "Is this something these people want to know?" If they don't want to know it, we're wasting everybody's time. I ask, "What exactly is it that I want to have accomplished when I've preached this sermon?" I need to chop out all unnecessary material. A sermon should be like a commercial budget when business is bad—everything in it must count for something or be cut out. When Norman Vincent Peale started preaching, his father asked him to send a ten-word telegram to him every Saturday night summarizing his sermon for the next morning.[53] Any sermon that can be summarized in ten words could probably be delivered in fifteen minutes and retain its essential message.

Listen to tapes of your previous sermons. Do you use verbal tics? The most common one is "you know." Eliminate it. It and others rarely fit.

Prepare a title that is less cute than informing. A simple title that lets people in on the topic helps the sermon get started before you stand to give it. Not tombstone titles, of course, like "On Worry." Too dead. How about "How Can a Christian Cope with Worry?"

Prepare for delivery. When the sermon is written, it is only partly done. Even as I prepare the sermon itself I say certain phrases out loud several times until I get them tuned to the ear. There's an important difference in what reads well and what sounds well. On Sunday morning, before anyone else arrives, I practice key phrases again, out loud and over the public-address system. They must sound out my meanings. I remind myself of what I mean to accomplish with my sermon that day. The best sermon is lost if the delivery is bad.

Some sermons will fail. A friend says he feels satisfied if two of his sermons a year are good. The rest have to be more ordinary. Maybe, but I'd hope we'd aim higher. It is comforting to know, though, that Babe Ruth struck out 1,330 times en route to his record 714 home runs.[54] Our sermons won't hit home every Sunday. Keep at it. Remember, it is important work we do when we stand to proclaim God's Word.

Perhaps the three-year seminary training that the disciples had was best. They saw their Professor touch people—physically and spiritually touch them. They saw him stand right in the midst of the crowd to speak freshly, fervently about his understanding of faith as it fit their problems and needs. They heard speaking that was based, always, on his best insights and his own diligent study of the Scriptures. They heard the Rabbi communicate in the vernacular. He was one of them. They saw him change people. They watched him begin to change the world. He was some preacher!

WEDDINGS

Weddings provide an opportunity for great celebration. The church assists, appropriately, in this celebration of joy. Here are some ideas.

I choose not to be the judge regarding who should or should not marry. If my schedule will permit it, I accept every request to perform a marriage. I can do more good helping a couple do well what they are determined to do anyway than I could by turning them away. It has been a great tool for evangelism. Few weddings fail to bring someone new to our congregation on a continuing basis.

I make it clear that I have certain expectations. I have a

fee—except for members of the congregation, who are already paying my salary. The service, if held in the sanctuary, will be a Christian service, including Scripture, sermon, and prayer. A small wedding in the office or elsewhere will include Christian prayer, at least. If one member of the couple being married is not a Christian, I will not ask him or her to use the words "God" and "Christ" in the vows, but I will expect the Christian partner to use them, and I will use them.

It is inappropriate to refuse to budge on details for the wedding. In most cases, I've found that once I've shared my rationale, most people are willing to go along with my design. If not, we work on changes acceptable to each of us.

If the couple is willing, we spend time discussing things that commonly cause trouble in a marriage—alcohol, in-laws, finances, loneliness, sex. I encourage Christ-centered life to assist a more fulfilling marriage. There is no point in requiring premarital counseling if the couple doesn't want it. To require it is usually to make captured couples jump through our hoops. I've found that few people learn what they don't want to know. So I offer premarital counseling. Most accept. Then it is on a more willing, fruitful basis.

The couple is asked to have everyone at the rehearsal who will have anything to do, including all ushers. At the rehearsal, when everyone is present, we gather for a few moments of orientation. I introduce the organist and myself to the group. We talk about why weddings are held in churches. If one of the persons being married is part of the congregation, I will say things like: "Lauri was baptized on this spot, she was instructed in the faith in the classrooms of this church. It is appropriate and meaningful for her to make her important marriage promises here." I tell the group that we will go over every detail to help assure a service that will be a beautiful memory for the couple and will enable those present to worship God. The group is informed that it will be a worship service. They will be helping to lead the service.

I tell the group that there are many valid ways to do

weddings. Some of the group have been at beautiful weddings that were done differently from the way we'll do it. They are not to think that I imagine my way to be the only way. It's just that my way is the best way I know of making it beautiful. Also, somebody has to be in charge of the rehearsal so we can get done. I'll be the director and proceed my way. If anyone knows of doing some detail a better way, I encourage him or her to describe it. We'll consider it. I've developed some of my favorite procedures by picking up on suggestions made by strangers at wedding rehearsals.

We begin the actual rehearsal with prayer, asking God's presence in what we do in preparing for a meaningful service the next day. Then we rehearse. I start with the ushers. Ushers are often the most difficult group to deal with. They rarely realize their importance—they think they don't need to be at the rehearsal. They think all they have to do is lead guests to pews. I show them how to offer an arm to the women. We decide who will seat the mother of the bride. We practice the means of ushering people out after the wedding (unless the bride and groom choose to usher their guests out themselves).

I tell them:

1. Seat people up front, filling each pew. If we're going to get together for a wedding, let's *get together,* up front, where the wedding will be. This is the hardest thing for ushers to do. They weaken when people come in and angle for the back pew. I tell the ushers, to *expect* people to follow. Don't say, "Would you follow me?" Say, "Please follow me!" And if necessary, "We've been asked to seat everyone up front." At the wedding I often observe and gently assist the ushers for the first few minutes to be sure they are doing all this.

2. Help the people in the room keep the quiet, preparatory mood the organist's prelude is meant to create. Do that by keeping the doors to the sanctuary closed rather than propped open, and by greeting friends with hushed tones rather than with glad shouts.

3. Be the room managers during the service. If, for

example, windows need to be opened, sense it and do it. Be on hand at all times, ready to respond to any need.

Next I have all the persons in the wedding party come forward to the spots where they will stand when the processional ceases. I put a nickel-sized sticky-backed round dot on the carpet where each is to stand. (Those dots stay there for the wedding. There is no confusion about where to stand.) Then we practice processing to those spots. I encourage male attendants to escort female attendants down the aisle. Escorted entries seem to me more natural than segregated entries. We rehearse the vows, the other chancel-area moves, the exit—and we're done. I inform all of the wedding party that at the actual ceremony I will tell them everything they have to do as we are doing it.

At too many weddings the guests attend a ceremony during which they can see only a row of backsides. People can't see the wedding they came to see. I arrange the wedding party to allow people to see the ceremony and to see the more attractive side of the attendants. I have the attendants stand forward of the bride and groom, to my back, facing the bride and groom and facing the congregation. People like the difference.

Three keys to weddings which will help minister to people are: (1) lead without being dictatorial; (2) make the rehearsal fun—an event in and of itself; and (3) make the wedding personal and light—in the sermon use names, give practical advice, and add bits of appropriate humor.

FUNERALS

I enjoy funerals. They are wonderful opportunities for binding a family together and for providing an opportunity for faith to grow.

They can also be wasted. Sometimes funerals are little more than dreary disposal services. Instead of celebrating the gifts of life—love, death, and hope—they become dead themselves. They often take place away from the church, where the Christian community usually gathers to praise God. They are marked by drawn faces, even on the pastor. They are filled with long, meaningless poems delivered in tones hushed as if normal voice levels were somehow forbidden. The name and life of the deceased, if mentioned at all, is mentioned only in the obituary. The sterility of such a service brings to mind the story of an acquaintance of mine who went to the funeral of a dear friend and never realized until she saw the body in its casket after the benediction that she was at the wrong funeral.

The funeral is most helpful when it is personal, thankful, and hopeful.

Personal. Omit the verbalized obituary if it is possible to have it printed on a worship bulletin. That may seem less personal, but a spoken obituary sends data and detail past the listeners' ears too rapidly to be helpful. The printed obituary allows people to read and absorb the details at their pace. The folder becomes a good piece to mail out to friends and loved ones who could not attend the funeral. In my first parish I talked the local funeral director into printing the obituary in the place where he usually had poetry, on the back of his handout folder. It was so appreciated by people that it became the practice throughout the town.

In addition, I use the name of the deceased several times during the service. I mention several admirable things we can all enjoy remembering about the deceased. That's possible with even strangers and scoundrels if you visit with the family of the deceased before the funeral. There is no need—indeed, it is inappropriate—to draw attention to the shortcomings of the deceased. Every man and woman is in some way God's gift to the world. Draw attention to those gifts. Be personal.

Thankful. Give thanks for the gift of love which "Maxine" wrapped around her children—for the ways in which she served the community and the church. Give thanks for the gift of death and, when appropriate, for the release it brings from months of pain.

Hopeful. The service should offer hope. There is reason to hope even in the most tragic deaths. Find it. Say it. Help the people feel less despair and greater hope. Help restore and strengthen faith. When my friend's nine-year-old son was killed in an accident, he said at the funeral: "I appreciate all the ways you folks have shared your love with us. We will miss Andy. But I want you to know that Andy's full life was not cut off. Full life cannot be measured in numbers of years. Our Lord was only thirty-three. That's too young, too. But he led a life that could not have been any more full. Andy was nine. That's too soon. Sure. But Andy received all the love we could give him. He played baseball. He had friends. He did all the things boys could do. His life was very full. And now his next life will be full too. Andy is still in good hands. Andy is O.K." I share that in many funeral services. Sometimes I tell how my own father, who is dead, is unbound, let go, set free (much like Lazarus in John 11:44), and must be having the time of his life. I tell how much closer I feel he is to me, now that 150 miles no longer separate our homes. These and other words like them offer encouragement. And always, there can be a restatement of your belief in the resurrection and the love of God.

Many local funeral customs could be improved upon. But remember, people hate change. And people are more important than our ideas of how funerals ought to be better. I found it helpful to visit with the local funeral director to find out how funerals were usually conducted in that community. I started out doing them exactly the way the community was used to, but with my flavor (personal, thankful, hopeful). Only as my credentials with the community grew to be accepted did I venture, slowly, to make any changes.

I'll use one major change as an example of how to deal with changes you would like to make. I have a problem with placing the casket up front. It is inappropriate to make human remains the center of worship in a service designed to praise God. I find the box a barrier over which it is virtually impossible to impart God's Word when all eyes and minds are riveted on that overwhelming presence. Worse still when the casket is open. It's hard to compete with a cold gray nose.

One Sunday I had a sermon on funerals. I explained how hard it is to grow beyond the funeral standards previous generations have established for us, but that practices do nonetheless evolve. I described some old customs we had left behind and wouldn't want back. Then I asked if we could consider one more step: a different location for the casket.

It was important to make clear that no one had done the wrong thing in having his or her relative rolled to the front of the sanctuary in the past. No guilt-heaping. I explained, carefully, my rationale. I assured them that my suggestion meant no disrespect for the deceased. My dad would have hated being at the center of worship. Most of us prefer less conspicuous lives than that. I told them that I had asked my wife to leave my casket at the entrance in the event of my death.

It was important to offer a benefit. I pointed out that, with the guests viewing before the service and the casket already at the entrance, as soon as the service was over, the family could follow inconspicuously behind the casket and get into the waiting cars. There they could sit quietly, watching the guests come out of the church instead of the other way around. Better privacy for a conspicuous moment.

I told the congregation that this was a suggestion, not a requirement. Every time a death occurred, I would reexplain my rationale to the family, but if they still wanted the casket up front, that is where it was placed. People are more important than our ideas. It worked. People came to prefer my practice.

DEALING WITH THE BEREAVED

When somebody in the parish dies, go to the family immediately. If you are in another state when it happens, telephone the family immediately. Respond. Express concern. Don't delay.

Don't ask what you can do. They don't want to suggest to you the ways to do your job. Instead, tell them what you'd like to do for them.

I have prayer with the family. If the body of the deceased is still present, we hold hands in a family circle around the one they've loved, and we pray.

We talk. About the deceased. Don't avoid conversation about the deceased. Encourage it. Let people cry. I often say to family members, "Don't ever tell your mom 'Don't cry.' She needs to cry. Just love her and embrace her while she cries. Cry with her if you are moved to do so."

We write an obituary. I've found that in the first hour or two after the death it is a tremendous stimulus for good conversation about the deceased to be writing his or her obituary. I have never found it to be too soon or otherwise offensive.

I help the family decide on a funeral time before they call other relatives, so they can avoid the cost of repeated calls. I tell the family to be prepared for these and other things:

1. Casket selection. "Don't feel obligated to buy more than you or the deceased would really want or can afford."

2. Visitors. "Many people will come to see you. Some will stay too long. Feel free to excuse yourself for resting when you need to."

3. Casket bearers. I help them think about whom they want to ask to be casket bearers. There is a beautiful symbolism in having the deceased's children, whom he or she brought into the world, carry their parent to the grave—or the grandchildren, if they are old enough. Otherwise, choose close friends who are physically able.

4. Greeting funeral guests. I suggest that the closest family members stand at the door of the church to greet guests as they arrive for the funeral. My brother

and I did that at our father's funeral. It was a wonderful time. We enjoyed those opportunities to say "Thank you for coming to my dad's funeral." It helped set the tone. This was not a sad time.

The weeks following the funeral are important. Relatives and friends have returned to their normal worlds. The bereaved have not. They need some attention from the pastor. Keep in touch. Talk about the deceased again and again. Sometimes some straight talk is needed. The very day my father died an older widow neighbor came to see my mother. I'll never forget seeing her shake her finger in front of my mother and say: "Now, Angie, the biggest problem you're going to have is getting out into the world again. You have to decide. Decide soon. You can sit here day after day feeling sorry for yourself. Or you can get up each day, get dressed, do your work, and go someplace. Get out with people. One death in this house today is enough. Decide to live. It's difficult, but you can do it." A few jaws dropped at the frank advice. But it was some of the best ministry anyone performed for my mother during her bereavement.

One young widow told me: "People should have more guts. Be as honest as possible. Say as much as you can get away with without being cruel. Leave out half-baked answers that evade the real issues. Some people said things I didn't understand, things I even resented. But I understood later and respected them for it when I saw that it helped." Sometimes we just have to say: "Cliff, Sarah is dead. Your head knows it. Your heart won't accept it, but Sarah is dead. No one can change that. She's O.K. But you're not. You won't be O.K. until you admit and say the words 'Sarah is dead,' and then get out and do something significant for somebody. Go to work. Don't sit here 'hermitizing.' You may hate me for it, but I'm going to push you until you come alive again." We're in the resurrection business. Sometimes we have to order as Jesus did, with a loud voice, "Lazarus, come out!"

It's hard work. It is normal for acute manifestations of grief to occur and recur for about a year. Two kinds of death seem to be the most difficult for survivors to cope with: an angry suicide directed at them, and the death of a child from age eighteen through twenty-five. They can lead normal lives again, but they will carry the pain of their loss around for the rest of their lives.[55] Help them.

When a minister friend of mine wrote a letter to my wife after her father's death, I learned the value of letters at such times. He said:

> I just heard of your father's death. . . . I remember hearing some of the things your father did for folks and how they appreciated his ministry to them. How they will miss him. But it really is easier to see a good man die than a questionable one. Somehow my dad often seems close to me and he's been dead for five or six years now. I see him sometimes in the mirror and hear him sometimes in my voice. Our love for people—living and dead—is a very real source of strength because it stays when the pain is gone. And believing, as we do, that this life is "boot camp" for the bigger one, we Christians have an expectation that always accompanies death.[56]

Right on. Write a letter when a parishioner loses a loved one. People need to know that you noticed and that you cared.

COUNSELING

In my first parish I was disappointed to discover that most people who could benefit from counseling wouldn't seek it. The fear of revealing private matters seems greater in smaller communities than in larger ones. Even entering the pastor's office door "feels" conspicuous. Also, I soon realized that few forty-year-olds seek the advice of twenty-five-year-olds on any matter. I had to wait.

There are many good books on how to conduct effective counseling. Let me just offer a few suggestions.

I never counsel over an impersonal desk. I move to a chair to sit nearer the counselee. I try to make certain the counselee understands God's gracious acceptance of him or her no matter how ugly the problem. I try to convey that message more by being gracious myself than by delivering ponderous paragraphs. I give opinions and advice. I find that most people *need* to know what I think and what I suggest. It's important that they and I both understand that I can be wrong, but I suggest ways to work the problem out. I do a lot of assuring. "It can be worked out."

I feel free to do a lot of probing. Often my opener is, "What event caused you to call me today?" I'll ask about other possible points of pain. "Is there any problem at work?" "Is there any problem in your sex life?" "Are there financial problems?" "Are you contemplating suicide?" It's like the physician who keeps poking at the possibilities. "Does it hurt here? Or here?"

And I do a lot of referring. I tell them that if the problem is going to require more than three or four sessions with me, it probably requires more skill than I have to offer. I suggest some therapists I trust. I never make the appointments for them. Counselees need to make their own appointments.

VISITATION AT HOME AND HOSPITAL

The issue of visitation is a gut-grinder for many pastors and their congregations. Pastors tend to put visitation low on their list of priorities and last on their schedule—maybe even squeezed out. Congregations, especially smaller, more rural ones, yearn for more of it. For many congregations, visitation becomes the decisive issue.[57]

Some pastors feel that visitation is menial, meaningless work, that their abilities are badly used "just holding the hands of little old ladies." I found that feeling to have been one of my biggest mistakes in my first parish. I needed to pay much more attention to the elderly and infirm.

Part of the problem seems to be the image of the word "visit." I hear pastors say they don't have time for chitchat, for just "visiting." I agree. The issue can be resolved when we turn the visit into a fact-finding mission. Of course, "friendly, personal chats" are exactly what most lay people say they want.[58] Yet it is honorable for you to have additional objectives in mind. What may be chitchat to the parishioners may to you be getting to know the main hurts and joys of the parish (fodder for helpful preaching), checking pulses regarding programs you have in mind, estimating (and shortening) the distance between pulpit and pew. Every visit can result in significant data-banking for effective ministry to the whole congregation. Done that way, visitation can be meaningful for all parties involved.

Give consideration to thoughtful timing of calls. Few homemakers appreciate morning visits. That's chore time for them. Avoid awkward times. For example, I know of a case in which a pastor and his wife regularly drop by unannounced just before noon and evening mealtimes. Parishioners were trapped. Anger! Try 2 to 4 P.M. and 7:30 to 9:30 P.M.

Make appointments. I find it awkward to phone for appointments myself. The phone conversation often turns into the visit that needs to happen in the home. So I have a volunteer or a secretary make those calls. She says: "Keith is doing some pastoral calling tomorrow. Would it work for you if he came to your home at two in the afternoon? He'd plan to be there about forty-five minutes."

I don't always pray during a visit. I do whenever there is some evident problem in the family, or when I feel it would be especially appreciated by a family. For some families there is special value in experiencing prayer together with their pastor in their home. In a visit with the ill and hospitalized, prayer becomes significantly more important, especially at the first visit during an illness. But whether in home or hospital, when in doubt, pray.

I found that caring was communicated more effectively when I reached over to take the hand or touch the forearm of the patient during prayer. There is a great deal of scriptural evidence concerning the power that is inherent in the touching of persons who are ill. The best prayers are those which simply address the main issues facing the patient—for example, fear of surgery or death, ease of pain, hope of healing, thanks for good tissue reports. Use the patient's name in the prayer ("Lord, be present here with Kay. Heal her body. Ease her pain"). Prayer on succeeding occasions need not be new. It can repeat the same continuing concerns.

Previous patients tell me it helped when they heard me say, "You're going to be O.K." I nearly always say it. If someone has terminal cancer, I still say it. I may say, "Even if death comes, John, you'll be O.K."

I never invade a family's right to inform a patient of a terminal condition, but if I know a patient knows of it, I make sure we talk about it. I want that person to know that God's love is active in death as well as in life. If I think the person is uncertain whether the condition is terminal but fears it, I ask, "Peg, are you afraid you might die of this?" It has helped many patients to be able to talk and cry with someone about those fears.

Some pastors have done harm in hospital rooms. They've ignored rules for isolation rooms. They've pushed nurses and family aside in a hurried, self-important manner. They've personally diagnosed the patient in alarmist fashion, upsetting families and weakening the patient. It must have been some such afflicted patient who wrote:

> I lie tortured, my nerves screaming. The Rev. Prude paddles into my room, frowns at my paperback books, dismisses the pretty nurse, and whips out his Bible. O Lord, I asked for the Comforter—why did you send the Wet Blanket?[59]

The patient is a captive audience; be fair. The patient doesn't need sermons that pass judgment on any phase of his or her life. Right now the patient is sick. Focus on that, and on Christ's love for that person. If other agendas are covered, let it be only because the patient suggests them.

Someday someone is going to be angry with you because he or she was in the hospital and you didn't call. Sometimes we don't call because we just didn't get to it. (Then we simply apologize and try harder the next time.) Sometimes we have a bad cold and have no business carrying germs to weakened patients. (Then a phone call helps—explain the bad cold.) Often, we don't call because we simply didn't know the patient was a patient. No one informed us.

There are reasons the minister may not know someone was in the hospital. Some parishioners want secrecy or privacy. Some truly feel we're too busy. Some people know that theirs is an "in today, out tomorrow" case—too small to matter. Many simply forget to tell us because they are preoccupied with their illness. And finally—here's the tricky one—some people are testing their importance in the parish and their importance to you as pastor. They want to see how quickly other parishioners get word to you and how quickly you respond, if at all. They are angry or hurt when those tests come back negative.

We may want to react defensively: "If you told your physician you were sick, why couldn't you have extended the same courtesy to me? You didn't make your physician guess! Why did you make me depend on E.S.P.?" Those may be good questions to use in a thoughtful conversation with the congregation about your need to be informed. But when you are dealing with an angry or injured person, the most helpful, pastoral, healing response may be to deal with the wound rather than the logistics that led to the wound. You might say: "Yes, I can imagine you felt ignored. I would have too, if I had been you. I'm really sorry. I would have wanted to call on you if I had only known."

Inactive Members

There are two categories of inactive members: the long-standing inactives who rarely cast a shadow against the church door and those who have been active but are in the process of becoming inactive.

Every member has reasons. He or she may never have been assimilated into the life stream of the congregation. He or she may have burned out. For some people, church may not be their thing—they joined just to see if it would be, or as a favor to an enthusiastic friend or employer. Others may tend to focus on certain pastors or programs, and they opt out when either changes. Some use foot power to register their votes—they walk out to "tell" you something, something about you, the congregation, or the denomination. A few have noses bent out of shape over a joke misunderstood or because their names were accidentally left off a list of workers. Some are project-oriented, so that when the project is over (for example, the building program, getting the kids through church school), they're done. Some simply have calendar conflicts—they work on Sunday mornings.

It is helpful to adopt an attitude of understanding about the reasons even though they may seem inadequate. It rarely helps anyone's life to be blamed or castigated for inactivity.

There *are* some things to do. The main thing I've tried to do is to do my church work as well as I can—doing the preaching, caring functions, and leadership things efficiently, thoughtfully, and thoroughly. If I do the best I can in those matters, I need not feel guilty about the persons who choose not to experience my ministry. I try not to blame them or me. I just accept the fact that my abilities and attitudes cannot meet the needs of everyone.

If someone who has regularly attended is suddenly absent for four or five Sundays in a row, and you feel sure it was not a vacation period, make personal contact with that person. Ask: "Is there anything going wrong between us? Is there a change of family or employment status we can help with? We miss you and don't want to lose you." Sometimes you'll get the truth. Sometimes not. Some will get back on track. Some won't. If you find that there was an injury in your relationship, a letter of apology or concern may effect repair.

If I find that there has been a change in a person's theological perspective and that it no longer coincides with the one expressed at our church, I try to help that person to a better understanding of our perspective. I caution the person as lovingly as possible if he or she is moving into a theological camp I consider destructive. Otherwise I respectfully suggest churches that might serve the needs of the member. People need to eat at tables where they are fed. I want them to know that God works in congregations and denominations other than our own, and that a membership change in search of more helpful ministry is quite acceptable.

Dealing with members who have been inactive for a long time is different. I visit each one personally early in my term as pastor. They don't get top priority—those who have remained active and those who are ill need my attention first. But I want the inactive members to get to know me. Then they can decide if I'm the sort of person who might make their reentry possible. I ask them if there is an old injury or any awkwardness which they'd feel comfortable discussing; maybe I can help. In those discussions, I avoid passing judgment on any actions of a former pastor, but I try to recognize the hurt the member may have felt. I encourage conversation, which helps to bridge the gap and may enable an unembarrassing return. If it doesn't work, I don't worry about it. But if it does and that day of reentry arrives, I simply say, "Good to see you, Dan. Come again," and draw no more attention to his presence than that. He may feel too conspicuous—and therefore awkward—to deal with glad-handing and ovations.

Some, however, prefer not to be on our rolls—or on anyone's. We don't like that, but that's what is real. So once a year we advise all the members that we need to know whether they wish to continue their church membership for the coming year. We include a copy of the vows everyone took when he or she first joined. Everyone who indicates a desire to maintain those vows and extend them for another year remains on our rolls. Those who do not wish to continue for another year are erased from the rolls. Some people need a way other than death or transfer to get off the rolls of an institution in which they no longer have any interest. We offer such an opportunity.

For those who want to be a part of our congregation, there must be meaningful ways for them to "get on board." They must feel as though they belong, so we provide many opportunities, including social, study, work, and worship, where people can move from the fringes to the inner circles of the life of the congregation. We want them to feel "in."

EVANGELISM

For me, evangelism is that work of the church which seeks to bring people into its life and membership. There are some important lessons to learn from Acts 2. One is that effective evangelism must begin with a good dose of God's power—his Spirit moving our spirits. Another is that evangelism requires getting our act together—getting up out of our lethargy and making deliberate moves to share the good news of the risen Lord.

The first step toward becoming a congregation that attracts people is to work on the quality of the life of the congregation itself. No evangelism program will ultimately work if people are asked to join a church that does not demonstrate a genuine commitment to Jesus Christ as Lord, nor will it work if the congregation does not exhibit warmth and friendliness. If these conditions are absent, the next suggestions won't work.

The next step is to empower the congregation to tell your story. Every time new people join our congregation, the officers and I ask each new member three questions: "What brought you here the first time?" (How did you find out about us?), "What kept you coming?" and "What, if anything, did you find disappointing or discouraging about this church?" We learn many things. The answers have a lot of similarity, providing reinforcing support for former policy decisions, giving guidance for new policy considerations, and simply informing new officers. But the most marked piece of information we get is that more members are brought by the recommendations of current members—happy ones—than by any other way.

The second most common thing that brings people is the advertisement in Saturday's newspaper. Newcomers especially mention being attracted by special words in the ad that locate the area of the church ("Northwest Omaha") and also by the words that suggest the age and style of the congregation ("Young, growing congregation. Casual dress encouraged"). I'm impressed at how often the words "young," "growing," and "encouraged" have brought people to our church.

The third thing that most commonly brings people to our congregation is the boxed-in advertisement in the Yellow Pages. It contains much of the same information found in the newspaper ad.

The most crucial element in evangelism remains the quality of life experienced in the congregation. Once people get to the church, keeping them there is the next job. That is part of getting the act together.

The pastor sets the tone. Honest, open friendliness that offers itself unasked. People will not spend much time trying to bring out your friendliness. Offer it. Engage people in good joshing, chitchat, warm handshakes, "good to see you's," and people will begin to do that to each other. Keep urging people to greet one another. Urge them to aim toward the visitors just to say: "Hello, I'm Jean Mulford. Glad you came."

Other things help too. I stand at the church door to greet people as they arrive, as well as when they leave. I study the names of last week's visitors so I can call them by name if they come this Sunday. If I can't recall a name, I say: "You were here last week. Can't recall your name. Give it to me again." Even recognition of previous attendance helps. I always write a handwritten letter to each first-time visitor. It is a letter designed to welcome them, to invite them rather than to rush them. To offer something to them as much as to urge something of them. It usually goes like this:

> Dear Barb and Wally—
> I'm pleased that Glenda and Chuck Staff invited you to our church, and that you came to worship God with our congregation last Sunday. Come again, often.
> Feel free to call on me if I can ever be of any pastoral help to you.
> God bless you!
> Sincerely,

I call on visitors who have attended three consecutive Sundays or so—long enough and regular enough to indicate significant interest.

But most of all, a church deeply committed to Jesus Christ, preaching that commitment and practicing rich, open, friendly relationships, will be doing the best evangelism. It will grow.

Congregational Involvement in Mission

There are two primary forms of the church's life: the gathered community and the scattered community. In many ways the gathered community exists to draw together support and resources for the community in its scatteredness—to empower the members for their mission and ministry out in the weekday world.

Any church that exists primarily to protect and savor its own existence is flirting with death. The best way to turn a dead lake into a live, fresh one is to create an outlet for its dammed-up water. Many ministers have found that the best way to breathe life into a listless, dying congregation is to help it begin to lift its focus from its own nave and navel to the world of others in need. A congregation that steadily grows in its determination to give away mind, muscle, and money for mission work in the name of Jesus Christ will be blessed with life.

The first requirement is an evident, persistent (not pushy) commitment to mission on the part of the pastor. The pastor needs to find the simple, but real ways in which the congregation can meet some human needs right in the immediate area. As that begins to work, the congregation can grow to finance some of the denomination's mission work worldwide.

It takes a lot of energy, interpretation, denominational loyalty, and praise for progress to make mission support and action a part of a congregation's life-style. But it pays off in congregational spirit and a greater commitment to the church's reason for being.

Social Concern and Action

Jesus was socially active. He urged his followers to address the issues of the poor. He struggled with the structures and mind-sets of his society. He took action in opposition to the commercial fleecing that occurred in the shops surrounding the Temple.

Now, years later, few if any church people would question the importance of the church's voice raised in support of anti-child-labor legislation or in opposition to Hitler. Those were O.K. But when it comes to involvement in current public issues, it is often thought to be meddling. As frustrating as that may be, it is normal. Hardly anyone can react reasonably when his or her own vested interests are questioned or attacked.

Pastors have to lead congregations into social concern and action carefully, thoughtfully, lovingly, slowly. Pastors list "to challenge secular values in present-day society" among the top ten of fifty-three issues for the church's life. But members list it as number twenty-five.[60] Any pastor who fails to understand, even appreciate, that difference will do some hurting.

This may sound as if lay people do not want the church to speak out on important issues. But "this is just not so for the bulk of American Christians. . . . Eighty-eight percent of the clergy and seventy-one percent of the lay people . . . feel their denominations should speak out on current social issues."[61] Congregations need and want to know where their pastor stands on issues, but they also want to know your biblical rationale for your stand. They want to retain the freedom not to adopt your stand without risking the loss of your respect. They don't want to be pressed and pressed and pressed with the demands of the gospel without a balanced mix of the comforts of the gospel.

I keep a couple of rules that work for me. One is that I will declare myself. But I will do so clearly, defining my biblical support, and in ways that *offer* my opinion rather than impose it on anyone. I get farther that way.

My second rule is that I will not normally position myself miles ahead of the congregation. (Remember, the general who places himself too far ahead of the troops will be mistaken for the enemy and will receive fire from his own troops.) If the congregation begins to fire at me, I am dead. My leadership capacity will have disintegrated. So I state my case clearly and with conviction—but not often. A congregation will not be inspired to bring peace to the world if I have declared war on that congregation. I choose to lead with love. Augustine said, "One loving spirit sets another on fire."[62] That has worked well for me in leading congregations to new awareness and action in significant social matters.

CHURCH OFFICERS

Some church boards actually make decisions. Others rubber-stamp or otherwise react to the decisions the pastor has already made. Others simply endorse parishioner popular opinion.

A wise pastor works in a collegial way with the congregation's officers. Several obstacles can get in the way. The pastor may be intimidated. I recall that my first meetings with officers were awesome events. At my very first meeting I was supposed to set the agenda, give direction, and act as moderator. At age twenty-five I felt like a teenager presiding over a group of seasoned church workers—several of the community's wise and leading citizens.

I made a decision—to be a leader too. These people had chosen me and were paying me to give them leadership in matters of spirit, worship, and mission. I would do so, expecting them to contribute their wealth of experience and wisdom as well. I would expect their forgiveness when I made my foolish errors, just as I would forgive them for what sometimes would appear to me to be stubbornness or sheer resistance. I simply behaved that way among them. We trusted each other. It worked.

I found out that refusals by officers rarely meant rejection when I dealt with them openly, freely, and in a leading way rather than in a demanding, authoritarian way. I found out that when I made a major proposal a no usually meant a maybe. They needed more time to think. I found out that when I came well prepared with feeling-level rationale, the responses made the "no to maybe to yes" journey quickly.

Officers with whom I've worked seem to work better when they have fun as a group. That may mean occasional social gatherings specifically for the officers and their spouses. But more important, it means that they need to have a good time at their regular meetings. We almost always have a lot of good joshing and joking at meetings of the officers. Laughter is a tremendous agent for providing ease, freedom, and unanimity, as well as acceptance of opposing positions when they occur. One pastor I know has a sack-lunch gathering of his officers every Friday noon. They can't all make it every Friday. They may or may not conduct a little business. But they develop into a wonderful support group.

It is helpful when at least some meetings include the pastoral question, "Is there anything any of you would like to bring up?" It indicates respect for their opinions and concerns.

The matter of officer selection is important. It is unwise for any pastor to name any of the officers, but it is also unwise for the pastor to have a total hands-off policy in the nomination process. I always meet with the nominating committee. It is important that the committee understand that I will not deny their freedom to nominate whomever they wish, but I also make it clear that it is my responsibility to raise a confidential red flag regarding certain persons whose names might begin to surface. It is also important that I offer several names for consideration. I never offer fewer than five names for every position open. And I often suggest the names in connection with the kinds of strengths and skills currently needed on the board. My purpose is to assure committed talent on the board as well a fair spread of ages and sexes.

Church officers should be helped to understand that they are called to lead. Weak boards tend to feel the pulse of their constituents and legislate in support of the pulsebeat. Those officers follow the congregation. Stronger boards lead their congregations. They create the pulsebeat.

COMMITTEES

The wise leader helps committees keep focused on their work. What are we going to do? How? When? Who?

Size makes a difference. Five to seven persons are usually plenty. Large committees cease to work as committees. Too many members are able to remain silent, and the group soon allows a dictator to make its decisions.

Pastors often get in the way of committees. By failing to delegate responsibility to committees, a pastor seems to say, "I'll do it myself because I can do it quicker and better." The pastor then defeats his or her own purposes by failing to develop among the committee members the capabilities they need to be effective.

MEETINGS

Any minister who hates meetings may need to look for another career. Meetings are nothing more than gatherings of people intent on accomplishing something worthwhile. Meetings are, however, the third largest time waster.[63] The pain occurs when nothing worthwhile seems to get done. There are ways to correct that.

Realize that some meetings are social events burdened by business. I love social events with friends, but I have had gut grinds when I've sat for twenty minutes of business stretched into two hours by unrelated frivolity. When I finally realized the importance of the socializing, I urged the chairperson to organize in such a way that the business could be taken care of quickly and efficiently. Then those who could stay were free to enjoy the rest of the evening. We were all happier. Another possibility is to schedule meetings only at an hour when people will need to get to the point and move on. In the business world, that time occurs at 11:30 A.M. and at 4:30 P.M. In the church, that may be right after worship, over lunch on a weekday, or maybe at 7 A.M. on weekdays. Never call a meeting when key leaders will have to be gone. Skip a monthly meeting if there is little to do. And keep it short. Meetings that last over one hour decline markedly in effectiveness.

If you have trouble getting people there on time and keeping them there to the end, put the most interesting items at the beginning and end of the agenda. Spend most of the time on the more important matters, otherwise time will be spent on items to be discussed in inverse relation to their importance. I know of a church where the agenda called for consideration of a $350,000 annual budget. It took fifteen minutes. An officer brought up a concern about the quality of paper towels used in the restrooms. That took thirty-five minutes. Try to assign greater time to program and mission than to finances and facilities. Put the items that need to take more time first on the agenda.

Prepare to report proposals so clearly that confusion and anger are avoided.

Know before the meeting begins what the meeting is to accomplish (or have the group decide that first, and quickly). Help the focus of the meeting remain on that purpose. When the purpose is achieved, adjourn.

Keep the temperature down. The best meeting room temperature is 66 to 68 degrees. It will help the meeting move more quickly.

Room arrangement is important too. Long conference tables are popular, but killers. They encourage groups to disintegrate into small pieces. Two church banquet tables placed end to end is the worst arrangement. Horseshoe shapes are as bad; they often put people's backs to each other. Two, three, four, or more banquet tables placed side by side to form a large solid-top square offer a much better arrangement for collegial conferences. Round and oval tables are the best shapes. I avoid any arrangement that leaves a hole in the center. The hole is very separating. The solid top seems to create less of a gulf between participants. And unless it can't be avoided, I let no one sit in a second row behind the other persons present. For real participation everyone needs to be at the table or in the same circle.

STEWARDSHIP

The theology of stewardship correctly includes the assignment of one's total life resources to the Lord's service.

However, lay leaders usually think of stewardship as being synonymous with money-raising or pledging the budget. We frustrate our lay leaders when we theologize about stewardship without helping them generate support for the church budget.

People vote with their feet and their purses. If they like what's happening in church, they attend and are willing to support. If they don't like what's happening, they stay away and withdraw their support. That's the first thing to remember in helping your church meet the budget for its mission and ministry. If attendance and support are problems, the pastor and officers may need to ask if people are being well served by what is happening in the church's life. Lack of interest and disapproval are usually sufficient to withhold support. However, interest, approval, and attendance may not always be sufficient to guarantee support. There needs to be a deliberate effort to encourage interested and attending members to underwrite the Christian work of the congregation.

The pastor will probably have to take an active leadership role in stewardship campaign design, implementation, and education. Four fifths of all pastors do.[64] By coincidence, one fifth of all pastors tend to be frustrated over the financial situations in their congregations.[65] They may be the same fifth who do not help generate funds in their parishes. Most pastors who avoid solid work with stewardship campaigns do so because they fear the subject of money. They somehow think lucre *is* filthy, or that the pastor must protect the purse of the parishioner. The parishioner will do the latter well enough. As a result of the pastor's reluctance, the work of the parish is impaired, and a good many people are never led to experience growth in the joy of giving.

If facing up to money-raising is difficult for you, then remember that neither Jesus nor Paul held back on the subject of assigning personal assets to mission and ministry. Jesus told his listeners to feed the poor; Paul asked the Jerusalem

Christians for mission support. They faced the subject squarely.

Second, seek help. Contact a nearby pastor known to be adept at stewardship. Ask him or her all the questions you can. Try your own ideas and designs on him or her. Attend stewardship workshops your denomination may provide. If there are none, attend some put on by another denomination you respect.

Here are some things that have been important and useful for me. Plan early. Most churches have their annual stewardship campaign in the fall to seek pledges for the coming calendar year. I like to plan the next campaign within two months of the last one, when its mistakes—and successes—are fresh in our minds. We set a target date for the campaign (usually the second Sunday of November), figure forward two or three weeks for follow-up, figure backward several months for preparation, and write a number of checkpoint dates into the plan. We state what each publicity piece will be, what their themes are, and when they will be done. It establishes when campaign workers will be secured and when they will be trained. And finally, the plan tells who will do each of these things. I find that it's important to involve as many people in the whole process as possible so that more people gain an interest in its success.

We've found it essential to put out lots of information about the campaign and its goals. People tend to give in response to what they perceive to be the financial needs of the church. We communicate those needs.

Five days before Campaign Sunday, a carefully prepared brochure is sent to every family. It is one we've designed and had professionally printed. It is designed to publicize the needs, to inspire, and to offer something (good Christian education, Bible teaching, pastoral counseling, etc.) as well as request something (your increased support on Campaign Sunday). It always has more photography than paragraphs. We include lots of photos of our parishioners participating in church events that occurred throughout the past year. We always include a photo of the pastor baptizing someone.

Related things happen in the pulpit too. Every Sunday of the year one of our lay people gives the congregation a one-minute report on something our church is doing in mission. The speaker indicates that we're doing that work in Christ's name, and then thanks the congregation for its financial support of mission. On the four Sundays prior to Stewardship Sunday, the speakers add, "We hope you'll increase your pledge on Stewardship Sunday so we can do even more of this kind of mission work next year—all in Christ's name." We choose our most effective lay speakers for those Sundays.

The Sunday before Stewardship Sunday, I always preach a "Here's What We're Doing in Mission" sermon. It tells in human-interest-story fashion a few things we're doing locally and worldwide to spread Christ's Word and love. I close with the request that everyone prayerfully consider substantial support on Stewardship Sunday.

Then on Stewardship Sunday I preach a sermon that proclaims the blessing of giving. I emphasize the value of tithing. I make it clear that I tithe, as does my wife. I've even chalked my personal figures on a board before the congregation and said: "That is the minimum that my wife and I plan to give away next year. One tenth before taxes. God is as important to us as our car. We figure that if we can afford a car payment, we can afford a God payment . . . [house payment . . . God payment, etc.]. Don't feel pressured by what we do; feel *challenged* by it. Move forward. Stretch yourselves in your commitment—even your financial commitment—to God this year. Start now!"

Right then we pass out pledge forms; time is given to fill them out. Then, to quiet organ music and congregational hymn singing we ask people to come forward—men, women, children—and place their pledge forms on the Communion table. Sound schmaltzy? It's effective. Then we dedicate the pledges with prayer. That afternoon, teams of callers visit the home of every pledging unit that did not hand in a pledge that morning. We keep making calls until all pledges are in.

That is a brief description of one way that serves well. There are other ways, but bear in mind that they will probably all require a few basic things: (1) a pastor who tithes; (2) a pastor who offers respectful and even enthusiastic support, assistance, and often initiative; (3) involvement of many lay people; (4) repeated telling of the stories of the church's mission; (5) a parish program and ministerial style in which the congregation has confidence and joy; and (6) leadership that clearly commits itself to the Word and work of Jesus Christ.

Budget

There can be great power in the use of money. It can be used to cripple a congregation or to lead it. The use of money requires a budget of some kind.

Budgets simply help a group set priorities and establish a course of action for a year. It's a way of saying, "Here's what we think is important to do . . . here's how much it will cost . . . here's how we plan to operate this year." The process of budgeting, then, becomes the point at which an organization's real values receive concrete expression. If mission is important or unimportant, the fact will probably be revealed by the weight assigned to it in the budget and by what its trajectory is in a row of years.

Budgets ought to challenge congregations. They need to grow just to keep the church and its mission adequate to meet inflationary factors. Growing budgets that are well interpreted urge congregations forward. I was telling our stewardship committee about a neighboring church that was suffering a severe shortage of receipts. Our committee chairperson asked if the church had a large budget. I said: "No. It's quite small for the size of the congregation." The chairperson responded with, "So there you are!" He was right. That would not always be the case, but often so. Budgets should lift the expectation levels of a congregation.

Sometimes we are surprised. In our church, on those rare occasions when the pledges oversubscribe the proposed budget, we feel that we have underbudgeted. We have underestimated the capacity of the congregation to underwrite the mission of the church. We have caught the congregation leading its officers rather than the other way around. Not so good.

It's helpful to demonstrate in the budget display that certain reimbursements to the pastor are *not* income or salary for the pastor. I've found it an error to list "auto allowance" in the "pastoral ministry" category. Some members add up the entire category and say, "Hey, he's getting an awful lot of money!" It helps to educate the congregation to the fact that an auto allowance is an operational expense. That educational process begins when the auto allowance is placed in the administrative category along with phone and postage.

COMMUNITY INVOLVEMENT

All Christians need to give away some of their own time and talents to communities of need beyond those they are paid to serve. It is one way of communicating a love and acceptance of the whole community.

Active service in the local chamber of commerce or a similar civic group can be meaningful. And a wider contact beyond the congregation offers other helpful relationships with people. It may also offer some excellent education about the larger life of the people you love and serve. My active work for the March of Dimes in the county of my first parish taught me a lot about fund-raising for church work. It also taught me a lot about a whole other slice of life in the community. It taught me several organizational skills, and it served the community.

A good rule is to spend as much time in community activities as the lay person is expected to spend in community and church work.

There are other guidelines. Don't forget who pays your salary. Don't let community activity pull you away from the fulfillment of parish responsibilities

4

GETTING ALONG IN THE PARISH

THE SPOUSE OF THE PASTOR

A woman in my first parish was perpetually angry with me. At one point she said to me, "There must be *something* good about you—Ruth married you!" My wife has eased my acceptance and assisted in many ways.

The reverse is sometimes true. There are wives who create situations like this: When you ask the minister how his church is going, *she* answers. She runs the choir. She demands attention. One wife I know required her minister husband to order the chairperson of the nominating committee to come to her house to explain why she had not been nominated as an officer of the church. This, and other actions like it, cost her husband his job. The congregation liked him, but they were weary of her overbearing insistence on being the real leader.

It is a complicated matter. The spouses of most ministers have alert minds and an active interest in the church. Many are very able persons whose abilities get buried. It is wasteful.

Not all spouses of ministers are wives, of course. Increasingly, some are husbands. That can be even more difficult. Congregations are not culturally equipped to cope with a male spouse in the pastor's home. To begin with, they have so few ways of celebrating their arrival. A tea perhaps? Welcome him to circle? There is a natural awkwardness that might cause the male spouse to feel lonely in the pew. Nevertheless, just as a congregation can come to love a female minister, so they can come to accept and appreciate the male spouse when his wife and he lovingly relate to the people and participate productively with them in the work of the parish.

Frankly, however, most spouses of clergy are wives, and more information is known regarding their situation. We'll address that side.

There appear to be three groups of clergy wives: (1) the spouse who almost seems like a co-pastor, who actively shares the pastoral function; (2) the family person, who feels the best help she can give her husband is to be an effective wife, mother, and housekeeper; and (3) the church hater or pastoral vocation hater, who may do her bit only out of love for her husband, or not at all.

The pastor's wife needs to have her needs met—to be fulfilled. She needs to enjoy the degree of involvement and recognition she desires, short of the point where it would harm the effectiveness of the pastor. That limitation is just as important as the old idea that we all have freedom to swing our arms until they begin to hit other people.

The expectations of today's pastors' wives vary little from those generations ago. They remain, primarily, to help advance the husband's ministry and to encourage the best interests of his "flock." The difference lies in the degree to which she allows herself to be wedded to and consumed by those expectations. Today's wife chooses not to have her life defined by those expectations.

My wife has handled it well. She is blessed with a comfortable fit in the community of faith. She has been able to be herself. She has never attempted to be regulated by the ghosts of the wives of previous ministers, never teaching the senior high class just because a predecessor did. Indeed, the rule my wife uses would serve most spouses well: Behave as any other interested lay person would. Cook at church dinners if you like to cook—otherwise don't. And so on. She remains her own person. When she decided to use her skill in secular employment, she did so with no sense of guilt about missing morning circle. When her schedule permits, she attends circle because she likes it and the women in it, not because she *has* to. She relates to the people of the parish well enough that members do not think she is rejecting them when she fails to participate in every event.

Employment is an important facet of life for many clergy wives. The majority now work for income. There is a growing acceptance of that. But still it is helpful if the wife can give some time to the church. A good rule of thumb might be for her to give the same amount of time to church work that might be hoped for from any other employed member of the parish.

The main point is that the congregation needs to feel accepted, considered, and loved by the spouse of the minister. If the members have that awareness, they will allow considerable leeway in what they expect of her. She sets the tone.

The quality of the marriage will also have a serious impact on the effectiveness of the pastor. The wife who is unhappy in her marriage will have difficulty delivering any of the support systems. Pastors, like most people, seem reluctant and slow about seeking adequate counsel for their ailing marriages. It is important to get excellent advice from a professional, quickly. More and more congregations are discovering that even divorce among ministers is better than hostility in the parsonage; it may be necessary in order to resolve the problems.

The Family

The pastor and his or her family, especially in small communities, live in more light than do most families. Ordinary characteristics and events are magnified by the goldfish bowl. Psychologist Dr. Thomas Osborne says that "unlike all other professionals, the clergyman and his family are supposed to reflect the 'should-dos,' while the rest of the world goes about in performance of the 'do-dos.' "[66]

That's one problem. Another is the amount of time the pastor has available to spend with his or her family. The average pastor spends about sixteen hours a week with family, even though he or she places it as a top priority. That's not much attention given to protecting a valuable investment—which a family is. Most church members feel they have adequate time to do things with their families, but most ministers do not have that feeling.

There is more on the issue of time in the section on time management in Chapter 3 and in the section on free time later in this chapter. Suffice it to say at this point that I find it important to take a regular full day off each and every week. Nothing other than funerals, death, or a true emergency alters that. And I confine my evening obligations to two nights each week. I've found that even the busiest pastors can do it if they decide to. They must be dedicated to family, and manage schedules rather than let schedules manage them.

When our family discovered the goldfish-bowl factor in ministry, we chose to be ourselves. We didn't declare war on customs, we just gently proceeded to live a family life we could enjoy. We've always had close friends in each community, and never have we hidden the fact. Some of the friends have been members of our congregation and some have not. We go out to eat with our friends when and where we choose to do so. When we run into other members, we greet them and chat a moment just as we would with a neighbor at the market. In ten years in our first parish we heard two criticisms about our having special friends. Each time I simply said to the congregation in a concerned tone (not an angry, scolding tone): "I've heard criticism about our having close friends. We can be *friendly* with all our parishioners but we can't possibly be *close friends* with everyone. I guess we just need to know from you whether we can have friends or whether we have to be lonely." Each time there was someone in the congregation who stood to say, "We want you to have friends." The congregation applauded. No more criticism.

For many people the pastor's family is assumed to be a model for how a family ought to be, and the pastor's children are expected to be models of good behavior. Be that as it may, *my* reason for trying to be a good father and husband is that I think it is best for my family and me. Any payoff for the parish is bonus, not motive. I instruct my children in good behavior for their own benefit. We simply try to be the kind of good family we'd want to be were I in any other kind of work.

Free Time

The Sabbath concept was not my idea. Check Genesis 2:2. Ministers often feel they never finish what they're doing, so they can't stop working. I figure that God knew what he was doing, that I can't outsmart him. I'll follow his model.

One of America's great preachers, Ernest Fremont Tittle, "died years before the actuarial tables decreed, and perhaps one explanation is that he echoed too faithfully Wesley's confession, 'Leisure and I have parted company.' "[67] Ministers are not the only career people who need to relax from work. Here is a matter of modeling I am quite willing to perform. Ministers do influence the daily life decisions and actions of their parishioners more by personal example than in any other way. I have found that my gentle but direct insistence on a regular day off each week and a full, totally work free vacation each year has caused some work-driven parishioners to relax more. They and their wives have thanked me for it. Still, the reason I take that regular free time is that it's good for me and my family. *We* need it.

The House

In many communities the church-owned house is a necessary courtesy in order that there be a place for the pastor to live. Though only 9 percent of the ministers' wives in my denomination say that living in a manse is a problem,[68] it does require patience. There are many hazards. Some congregations neglect the house they own. Those ministers in denominations with some kind of district superintendent can usually depend on their leadership to see to it that a congregation keeps the property in good shape, especially in preparation for the arrival of a new pastor. But when that does not happen and the pastor finds his or her family living in a deteriorating house, something should be done. We do no one a favor by playing the part of "poor Pastor Jones who lives so humbly."

Talk to the right person in your denominational structure. E. F. Tittle says: "I told my district superintendent that unless the saints could provide me a decent place to house my family he had my resignation. The saints did provide."[69] Adequate housing conditions have proven to be important factors in whether a minister can remain in the profession.

Talk to the right committee in your church. Don't explode. Don't belittle. Explain the problem without making your spouse out to be a complainer. Help the leaders understand that the condition of the house is discouraging to you and your family. Ask them how they can begin a steady program of improvement. Be careful, of course, never to complain about a manse that is already better than most of the homes of your parishioners. That's asking for war—a silent, cold-shoulder war.

Before I went to my first parish the congregation had done a nice job of readying the manse, but during my ten years there many more improvements needed to be made. Never once did any of those improvements happen without my asking for them. The congregation was excellent about responding helpfully to my requests, but the officers never took the initiative. We must sometimes take the initiative.

The largest request I made was for carpet. The floors seemed cold and bare. I knew it would be a large expense, so I

asked for permission to carpet those areas at my expense. I
suggested we assign a ten-year life to the carpet and that when
I would leave the parish I'd be reimbursed, on a prorated
basis, for each year of use we left for the congregation. We
would donate the cost for the years we used the carpet. The
officers seemed to appreciate the fairness of the proposal. It
made me seem less demanding. They proceeded to have the
carpet installed at the church's expense. Even with a different
outcome to that story, the proposal is one that can help bring
some comfortable appointments into the manse in a way that
doesn't pester the officers about what some would think of as
luxuries. I knew that some of my officers and parishioners
didn't have carpet in their homes. It would have been foolish
of me to insist that the church install carpet for my comfort.

One thing turned out less well. I felt a great need for a
garage for our car in those cold, snowy Nebraska winters.
There was none. I was beginning to prepare a cost analysis and
recommendation for our trustees when I overheard a member
say to someone else, "That preacher is always asking for
things!" He was one of the few people in the parish who didn't
have a garage himself. I was embarrassed away from the
recommendation. We never got a garage.

Were I to reside in a manse again, I'd seriously consider
recommending to the officers at one of our first meetings that
they adopt a plan for annual maintenance and improvement of
the house. It would establish that each year prior to
budget-planning time a committee would be named to visit the
manse. It would be composed of three persons, including at
least one male and one female. The committee would
recommend budget figures to accomplish whatever maintenance would be helpful in the upcoming budget year and to
provide for at least one annual improvement for the manse.
Such a plan would sound reasonable to many—maybe
most—church boards in the honeymoon period, and it would
reduce the level of frustration for many pastors and their
families.

Take good care of your home, especially its appearance. One of the messiest homes I've been in was the home of a pastor and his wife. It was a church-owned home. It was messy in and around the house. Outside Christmas lights were invariably still up in midsummer. The yard was junky. This was in a small town. Parishioners were embarrassed to know that the whole community observed the poor care. In addition to their shame, they grieved over the abuse that they felt was being inflicted on "their" house. It generated high levels of hostility toward the pastor's family. We must give at least the care and respect for a home that any landlord would want given to his or her house. We must keep the yard as well as any neighbor might want in order to maintain comfortable relationships with the neighborhood.

The problem is not always solved by pastoral ownership of the home. Another pastor I know embarrasses his congregation by his treatment of his home, even though he owns it. He painted it purple on the outside and let his yard go to high weeds. His congregation is embarrassed by being known in the community as "the church with the crazy preacher in that ridiculous purple house with a jungle around it." We have the right to do what we want. That's important. But we must always be aware of the cost of certain actions and certain inaction—we may lose a job. The feelings people have about their collective image in the community are usually normal and must be considered. There is probably a major difference in city living—few parishioners will know where you live, let alone that your house is purple. So they will probably care less.

THE SALARY OF THE PASTOR

Salary is a critical problem for many pastors and their families. Clergy are paid less than most professional people. Frustration! And their rate of annual increase runs only about two thirds the increase of other professionals. That amplifies the difference and the frustration. And although most churches conduct some form of annual salary review, fewer than half actually allow a cost-of-living adjustment to keep their pastor up to the same buying-power range they provided when he or she first came to the parish. More frustration!

We can do something about it. Not everyone wants to, of course. All around us are lay people who feel obliged to keep the pastor poor or to keep the pastor in a dependent relationship. Some genuinely feel that it is unchristian for ministers to be concerned about money. The basic problem, however, is not such attitudes. Kenneth Mitchell of Eden Seminary says: "The pastor himself or herself very frequently colludes in those problems. He or she lets them happen. The fundamental tacit contract is that the Christian attitude consists of being a passive patsy, and the pastor buys into that one over and over again."[70] When the pastor colludes, he or she often proceeds to unleash ill-advised and ill-disguised anger in sermons and in clergy confabs.

Some get second jobs. Indeed, 25 percent of ministers have second jobs to earn extra income, compared to 5 percent of the people in the general labor force of America.[71] There are a variety of reasons. But for many, the problem is that the pastor has not led the congregation to deal adequately with the salary question, so rather than confront the issue, the pastor sells siding or shoes on the side.

Let there be a warning for those who consider seeking additional employment: Be sure to discuss the matter fully with the church board. I know a minister who had a forty-hour job on the side for a full year before his congregation found out. When they discovered it they got rid of him. They felt taken. They felt lied to. They had become aware that he was seldom around. When they needed him and called, his wife would cover in ways that allowed parishioners to infer that he was at some meeting or on a hospital call. Church work wasn't being done. In effect, he had been stealing nearly a year's salary from them.

The best plan to try first is to confront the church board carefully and kindly with your salary dilemma. Lay out the problem. Ask for help in solving it.

For several years in my first pastorate I received very modest salary increases. It was mainly my fault. I secretly wished for more, but when some officer would say, "How about $200?" I'd say, "That's fine." I was losing in the inflation cycle. Finally one wise officer cornered me privately and said: "Look, Cook, don't be so quick to take such modest increments. Take the lead, or at least let some of us others take the lead before you so quickly accept the low, conservative suggestion." The next year I asked for $1,000 before anyone else said anything. I got it without a whimper.

At the first annual salary review in my second parish, I asked each officer to write out the annual salary of the major wage earner in his or her home (last year's total income for farmers and other self-employed persons). No names, just figures. I found that their average was 50 percent more than my salary, including housing. (*Always* include housing when discussing your salary—that puts you in an apples-to-apples conversation with other people.)

So then I made my little speech. "I work as hard at my job as I think you do at your jobs, and if I don't, you should perhaps fire me. . . . I work as professionally at my work as you do at yours, and if I don't, you maybe ought to let me go. . . . I spend as many hours at my work as you do at your work, and if I don't, maybe you should release me. I think I've brought the kind of results here at this church that you hoped for. If all of that is true, I'm wondering about the wisdom of paying me so much less than you get paid. You appropriately prefer that I live in the general area and price range of homes you live in. I think you want me to dress well too. I think you want me to send my children to college, just as you hope to. You want me to have some of the comforts you have, and to be able to mix in your company. If those things are true, then I need to have the kind of income level you, on the average, enjoy. It seems to me that if I must work closely, creatively, and confidently among you officers, I need to be more than the 'poor boy' in the group. Now, I know you can't budget to correct the difference in one year, but can you commit yourselves to a program of increments that bring us to a par? I will continue to work the best I know how in any event, but knowing my own humanity, I assure you I can work better if I don't have to feel discouraged about my disparate salary condition."

They agreed. In two years they had me at their average salary level and have done very well for me ever since. Clergy shouldn't be a privileged class, but it needn't be a pitied class. In order to care for that, the pastor may have to take the lead.

CONFLICT

Conflict is a fact of life. It isn't all bad. Often it is the anvil upon which good things are hammered into good shape. It is a device by which groups become involved. It is a way by which people give claim to common turf. Cared for properly, conflict creates intimacy. Those are benefits.

There are costs to conflict too. Honeymoon periods have a way of coming to an end, sometimes abruptly. In my first parish, the honeymoon period ended more by process than by particular events. I thought it was events. I thought they didn't like this or that thing I did or proposed. The truth was that more often the "thing" was O.K. What was wrong was that I went about it too quickly, too forcefully, without sufficient attention to feelings of readiness on the part of the people affected by the events.

I needed to be far more observant of congregational custom and comfort, arrived at after years, even decades, of development. The changes I proposed were usually correct in content but often incorrect in process. I often failed to bring people on board so that they also wanted to achieve what I wanted to achieve. So there was conflict that brought frustration and sadness.

Sometimes the conflict is with one powerful person. His or her power may not have an effective influence on church policy, but it may still be powerful in that it tears away at your time and temperament. One minister friend told me about his own particular "witch in residence." She assumed a position equal to enemy with the pastor. She never seemed to be aware of that; she thought she was just concerned. In fact, however, she rode his back so much that both he and the parish began to suffer. After many fruitless hours of trying to deal with her, he decided he had to squeeze her out of the parish in much the same way that cancer has to be removed before it destroys the whole body. Some people have a need to play the game called Clobber the Leader. Sometimes it helps all parties concerned to invite them to find another parish. This has to be done very carefully, of course, or the congregation that sympathized with you up to that point might now turn on you for "being so mean to that woman."

A woman in one of my parishes was like that. I found it wise never to confer with her alone. If she came into my office to talk things over, I'd immediately ask her to wait while I phoned a church officer to come over and sit in on the conversation. She didn't like it, but it helped each of us behave a bit better toward each other, and it also helped me to know that an officer could verify the accuracy of later grapevine reports of the confrontation. That very procedure provided solid board support when it finally did come to the point of removing such a person from the church rolls. The officers had viewed at close hand that member's acid accusations. They did not have to rely only on my reports.

Another way is to find ways to harness all the energy that person puts into his or her active opposition and put it to greater use. Divert it to pet projects for good that might fulfill some of that person's unmet needs. If effective, that person might turn into a tremendous ally. I've tried it. Sometimes it works, sometimes it doesn't.

Sometimes the conflict is caused by wide differences in what clergy and congregation think is important. There is far more to say about that than can be said here. Suffice it to say that the pastor must find out what is important to the congregation and deal with it respectfully, or the pastor won't be effective in interpreting what he or she feels is important. When a congregation's feelings are not recognized, and when what they think is important seems to be ignored, they withdraw their consent—and conflict follows. Blaming begins. Resignation in some form or another begins to occur.

And then, of course, some people just don't like you or me. It seems inevitable. For some it's because of genuine differences of personality or opinion. For others it may be that they feel so close and loyal to the former pastor that no one else could do. Still others have an emotional need to be done with church, to check out. There are people who can't do that without having a culturally acceptable reason. That reason may be an unhappiness or conflict with the new preacher. It is an age-old way of bowing out. It lacks grace, but it happens.

There are times, too, when the pastor becomes the lightning rod. He or she receives the jolts of anger when a congregation feels financial pressure or when people are upset at a denominational decision.

Here are some things to do:

1. Make use of creative avoidance. Titus 3:9 says it: "Avoid stupid controversies." Or as another old saying goes, "Never get into a stinking contest with a skunk. Even if you are right, you'll come out smelling bad." Take a close look at every potential controversy. Some wars aren't worth the costs. Stop them before they begin.

2. Avoid blaming. Resist pointing fingers, literally. Those pointed 45-caliber fingers have a way of going off and causing more trouble. Make a conscious effort when tense or angry to use full five-finger hand expressions rather than a pointed first finger. The body language expressed is far friendlier; it is less angry, less warlike.

3. Use ordinary good psychology. To start out with "You're

wrong" forces the opponent into a fighting corner. Better to start with: "I can see what you mean. I understand that feeling. I've felt like that too. But here is some additional information or insight that has led me to different conclusions." Then present your case. That approach stands a better chance of succeeding with less destructive conflict. Get the issue out on the table, but don't attack.

4. Take the initiative in getting the angry issue out and on the table. I recall having to lead a meeting with a group of very angry people. I said: "O.K., what are the issues we need to discuss before we leave this meeting? Let's get them listed on the chalkboard." I jotted down every topic offered, always asking every contributor if my way of listing his or her suggestion kept faith with the content of his or her concern. (That checking is extremely important. People need to know that I at least understand and reiterate their issue accurately.) When the list seemed to be complete, I saw that one significant item was missing. I knew it because of previous conversations. So I said: "I think there is one more important issue you may have found too awkward to verbalize. I think a lot of you are awfully angry with me for [naming the thing I'd done]." I saw several nods of agreement. I went on: "That may be the main issue. I understand and appreciate your reluctance, but we really need to talk that out fully too." The evening ended well. What I found out later from one of those present was that the one thing that helped most to bridge the gap had been my willingness to broach the angriest underlying issue, which involved me. Take the initiative, kindly but bravely.

5. Go to people you've injured, even if the offense is imaginary. Go quickly. Talk about the offense. Don't dodge it. Don't be overly defensive. Apologize. Many times I have gone to someone's home to say: "I've learned that you've been hurt by something I said. Can we please talk about it?" I always apologize. Even if I feel I didn't do anything wrong, I will at least say: "I didn't mean what you heard. I still feel I said the right thing for that occasion, but I can see that it

injured you. I apologize for not stating my case clearly enough to avoid that injury. I didn't want to hurt you. I hope you'll forgive me." If word of the injury has reached around the parish, I'm careful to report to the board at its next meeting my knowledge of the injury and my attempt to heal it, detailing the nature of my explanation and apology to the injured party. That way, if the person continues to voice anger, the board is apt to support me by saying: "We know he apologized. He tried. What more can he do?"

So, be in charge and guide the process. Leadership in conflict management means to be in charge of the process at hand without overcontrolling the people engaged in the process.

The best thing to do is to love. And forgive. Harry Emerson Fosdick spoke of several major conflicts he experienced in parish ministry, saying something that rules in every conflict for the Christian: "There are many opinions. . . . I am not (always) sure whether they are right or wrong, but there is one thing I am sure of: courtesy and kindliness and tolerance and humility and fairness are right. Opinions may be mistaken; love never is."[72]

Development of a support system is important for any pastor. My wife is a tremendous encouragement when I tell her my problems; she sometimes has vision that I lack. Other times, friendly colleagues in the ministry have given me their ears. In Chapter 3 I spoke of my "coffee-shop cabinet," that small group of wise, trustworthy, considerate members of the congregation. When I need to talk things over, I can call on them, singly or in groups, to chat. I say, "How about lunch today, Frank?" or, "Having a coffee break today, Neal? How about joining Francis and me?" I share a problem and get some tremendous pastoral help from dear parish friends.

The Crunch That Comes for the Congregation

"That new preacher is changing everything." People love improvement, they just don't like change. That's why all change has to happen either so subtly that it isn't noticed or with congregational consent after the members or their leaders have been persuaded that it will result in improvement.

In my first parish I made too many changes too quickly with too little educating, or with too little communication about the potential for improvement. I dislodged practices and principles that had been established and found useful over many, many years. There was naturally shock, dismay, discouragement, and often anger at my actions. People hate change. I needed to respect that fact much more than I did at first.

Congregations do have to put up with us—a passing parade of pastors, each wanting to change things that will only be changed again by the next minister. We may be there three years. The dust hardly settles when the next preacher whirlwind arrives to stir things again. It can be disabling for a congregation.

First, then, make changes slowly. Know the people, their needs, and their possibilities first. Work with *people* before you start in on program.

Next, make sure any change is worth the fuss and energy it will entail. Make sure the congregation can live with it now and that your successors can live with it later. Make sure the change is designed to meet the congregation's needs rather than yours.

Decide whether the change requires subtle, silent implementation or announcement, consent, and encouragement. I've done it both ways. Earlier I told of coming to my present parish where I moved the worship room chairs an inch each week. Not one person ever noticed. It helped make us a friendlier, more worshipful group.

I recently attended worship in a large church that was less than half filled. I listened to a friend preach. I found myself noticing the wide, empty spaces between the people in the pews and I thought about the extra energy it required of my friend to overcome the distances thereby created. I wondered how I might deal with that. Bolted-to-the-floor pews can't be moved an inch each week. There are many older people there; they learned to love their favorite pew.

I decided I'd probably have some careful conversations about the situation with key leaders. I'd get them on board. I'd call on several of the elderly women. (If the older women in a congregation are on your side, you can do wonders. They like being considered, and they often wield a great deal of influence.) Then some Sunday I'd say something like this: "Friends, I need your help. If you were to invite some friends over for dinner some evening, you would never seat them at a large table, each person ten feet or so apart from the other. The dinner would be a disaster. Real communication or communion couldn't occur. If you are going to get together, then you really have to get together. I too need to do that—here on Sunday mornings. I wish you knew how hard it is for me to preach over a gulf of empty pews up front. They separate you from me, and we're here to be together in the Lord. Let's leave the back pews empty if any need to be empty. Help me. How can we be a family in God's house, how can we commune or communicate God's love when we are so separated from one another? I really do understand that you have experienced years of coziness in certain locations, but please, let's get cozy with each other rather than with pews. I need togetherness to help God's Word and his way get across. Will you help me? Will you just get up this morning and come forward? Please. And if I ask the ushers to rope off the back pews from now on, will you honor that? We come together to worship God, now let's really do that. Let's come together. Thank you for helping me." It would work with many people who would willingly change if they thought it would really help.

That's education. That's communication that can pave the way for change without destroying a congregation.

The Crunch That Comes for Clergy

The pastor will sometimes have morale problems, will feel lonely, frustrated. He or she may have problems with self-worth or professional worth.

We've already talked about several of the common conditions that create these kinds of crunches for clergy: role confusion, financial stress, spouse and/or family dissatisfaction, and conflict. Isolation is often a problem. The school you attended can make a difference. Ministers who attend denominational seminaries are generally happier in parish work than those who attend interdenominational or nondenominational seminaries.[73]

Though it can come anytime, most ministers experience their greatest disillusionment and stress during their first year or two in the ministry. And it seems to stem most from a feeling of powerlessness. The church seems to have so little influence on society. We thought we were called to lead a mighty army of Christian soldiers eager to march onward but we find that we're chaplains to old warriors long since withdrawn from the front. We look at old scars and listen to old war stories. Powerlessness. We preach magnificent sermons, only to discover later that the folks still talk bitterly about "lazy niggers" and "cheating welfare recipients." Powerlessness. We're not getting God's good news through. They listen but don't hear. It can be discouraging.

It helped me, finally, to ask a few trusted friends if my ministry was having any impact. I asked them to describe any fruit of my work. I needed to know if I was serving a purpose. I discovered that I—and this would be true for nearly every minister—served a tremendous purpose in the community and directly affected the lives of many people. If we do our job well, we literally make life possible for some people. We bring the most important messages: God loves you, you are forgiven, you are worth something, Christ resurrects your life. Delivered well, those ideas and their accompanying messages change the lives of people more than any other professional person could do. I found it was important to hear the compliments that came—not to dismiss them, but to hear and savor them.

As for the disappointing responses of people, I remembered that the hardest job is to alter a person's attitude. It was tough for Jesus. So, too, for me. I'd have to love them along patiently. Realizing that is essential to our sanity. Those who have left the ministry tend to have rigid views of how people ought to respond.[74] When responses did not coincide with their views, these pastors were not able to adjust, relax, and keep working. Our work is legitimate. It is powerful. But we have to remain flexible and patient.

Similarly, there is the feeling that the congregation doesn't care. I have gone to unlock the church door in the morning and in a moment of despair have asked, "Does anyone but me actually care?" Very soon I found that *I* was feeling low and blaming the congregation. Now when I even start to feel that way I get out the membership list, read it, and ponder all the things so many people do. "There's Phil. He does so much around here. He cares. And there is Dorothy . . . Chuck . . . Earl . . . Betty . . ."

Some pastors feel strain and loneliness because of faith crisis. That is, the faith they feel compelled to preach is different from the one they feel developing—or failing to develop—within themselves. That requires at least two things: lots of prayer and lots of talking. Pray to God, and talk to your spouse *and* a trusted minister friend.

Some ministers feel trapped and lost in small-town parishes. Small towns can seem like islands of antiquity where we feel overtrained, underused, and therefore tense, terse, and trapped. I found, however, that both big towns and small towns have people of every degree of sophistication. The small town has its ugly sides and its wonderful assets, as does the city. We'll live and serve better in those smaller towns when we learn to love the people and enjoy the benefits of villagelike life. Those people have the same joys, sorrows, fears, and needs their city cousins do. Christ's love is needed there.

It *can* be lonely in a small town, however, if you don't make friends. So make friends. We did. See the section on family earlier in this chapter to read how we handled that. And even though the miles were sometimes many, we organized many welcoming dinners for new clergy and their spouses who were of our denomination and moved into our corner of our state. We had a similar dinner for every departing minister. We always attended, as did most of the other ministers and their spouses. We refused to be loners. We saw our colleagues. We had great fellowship. We excised the isolation by taking aggressive action against it.

When in despair, go work with people. Force yourself to call on people. Keeping in close touch with people is one of the best antidotes to despair.

BEING A DENOMINATIONAL/JUDICATORY PERSON

It has been my observation that the more effective pastors usually relate well to their denomination and its area judicatory or district. It's easy to play to the congregational grandstands—to appeal for popularity by fostering suspicion of the "big brother" element in denominational relationships. It's easy to use the denominational headquarters as a whipping boy.

I have sought to be active in area denominational work and have encouraged our church members to be similarly active. The result has been that our congregation's horizons have been lifted to larger mission and ministry.

DEALING WITH YOUR PREDECESSORS

There are two aspects to your relationship with your parish predecessors: your direct dealings, and the way you manage the shadows they leave behind in the parish.

Direct dealings. I assume that former pastors have a continued interest in the parish and therefore I leave every former pastor on the newsletter mailing list as long as they and/or their spouses remain alive. They are automatically invited and genuinely welcome to return for special congregational functions. If circumstances are appropriate, I contact them so they can preach at least one Sunday while I'm away on my vacation. The congregation enjoys the opportunities for reunion. When my predecessors' special friends in the parish die, I phone them to advise them. I invite them to make contact with the family of the deceased if they want, not as pastor but as friend.

Then there is the shadow that remains after the former pastor moves away. "Rev. Wiser-Than-You used to say . . ." Lyle Schaller makes the excellent point that the real predecessor may not be the pastor immediately before you.[75] A pastor a few pastorates back may have had such an impact on the parish that he or she is the main ghost that lingers in the hearts and minds of the people.

My rules. I never criticize any former pastor and his or her work. I never encourage others to describe a former pastor's faults, except in those cases where I determine that telling them is necessary for a healing process. And even then I tell myself that I'm hearing the words of an injured person whose vision may have been impaired. I try, in my response, to appreciate the injury of the parishioner rather than to confirm the "abusiveness" of my predecessor. I bear in mind that, after I leave, someone will be telling stories like that about me to my successor.

I publicly compliment the work of my predecessor whenever I can genuinely do so. I draw attention to the contributions he or she made. A former pastor's friends in the parish need that kind of recognition. Besides, it's deserved.

Beyond that, I simply do my job the best I can, knowing that I will lose some people who can't transfer their loyalty from my predecessor to me, but that others will return who were out before If I work in a diligent and secure fashion, the shadows begin to look like mine.

HONORARIUMS, FEES, AND DISCOUNTS

I began my ministry with a sure sense of righteous indignation about ministerial discounts, fees, and such things. I've mellowed.

Discounts for ministers are not common now, especially in larger communities. In my first parish I told each merchant who offered discounts that I enjoyed getting the best bargains possible but that I received a salary and would prefer not to receive an advantage most other people did not get. I recall one merchant who responded by saying: "Look, I've been giving discounts to ministers for decades. I'm not stopping now. You don't tell me how to run my business and I'll not tell you how to run yours." Mr. Harper kept his word, and I think I never again advised him regarding his business. I found out that it was best never to expect clergy discounts, never to angle for them, but to accept them graciously when given and say "thank you." I stopped being cynical about them.

I make it known that members of the congregation are never expected to pay me any fees for performing baptisms, weddings, or funerals. I tell them that is part of the pastoral ministry they help provide when they contribute to the budget of the church. Still, these same members often hand me a check after a wedding or a funeral. I used to try to hand it back. There was a courteous struggle. It was awkward. Finally one member verbalized the message the others had tried to convey. She said: "We know we don't owe it. You don't expect it. But we want to give it. It's a gift. Won't you let people who love you give you a gift?" Hazel had me. Now I simply say, "Thank you." They are truly honorariums.

Fees for weddings and funerals of nonchurch people are another matter. If you prefer not to charge a fee, a good thing to say is something like this. "My services for your wedding have already been paid for by the members of this church as a mission to you. If you want to help provide in some way for the future mission to other people, then find a way to contribute income or energy to this or some other church."

I prefer, however, simply and frankly to charge a fee for such services for nonmembers who do not contribute to the budget of the church. In our first conversation, I tell them that I charge a fee and that I would not mind their looking elsewhere if they object. The figures will change through the years, but at the time of this writing I charge $30 for a wedding, plus another $30 if there is a rehearsal. In former years I found that when I said "Whatever you want to give" in response to the question "What should we pay?" I usually got $10. The photographer at the weddings got $50 or more for one hour's work. Afterward he dropped off the film at the studio and was done with it! I felt I was at least as necessary to the occasion as was the freelance photographer. Few couples bat an eye. They seem to appreciate the straightforward approach.

PERSONAL DEVOTIONAL LIFE

The central crisis in ministry may be the crisis of faith. The disciples asked Jesus what they had to do to be doing God's work. Jesus responded, "This is the work of God, that you believe in him whom he has sent" (John 6:29). This becomes, then, the work of the pastor: to believe—in the presence of the people—in him whom God has sent into the world. And belief, like love, needs maintenance.

However, we have clergypersons who never pray except professionally. We have ministers who never study God's Word except to get a lead on next Sunday's sermon. You can get away with that in the ministry.

Let me suggest self-gain at this point. Pray sometimes just for the benefit of it. Read the Bible sometimes to discover personally the joy in it. The discoveries and integrity of it will empower you for more effective ministry.

STUDY—CONTINUING EDUCATION

Good shepherds do not continually force their sheep to eat grass that's too short. Some of us keep preaching from wells that went dry quite some time ago. Both continuous and continuing education is necessary. By continuous education I mean that daily diet of study which keeps us primed for our work. By continuing education I refer to those more obvious blocks of time (for example, a couple of weeks or a series of summers) that we assign to education for improved ministry.

Parish people generally respect a pastor's need for study. On the other hand, the same parishioners are likely to be frustrated when their minister devotes more time and attention to books than to people, or when he or she seems to be using parish-given time and finances to prepare for an alternate career, or when the study seems to issue in sermons that are basically collections of lengthy quotations from "all those books he reads." We do need study; we just need to avoid the tendency to find security in ideas.

One way to do that is to ask yourself how what you are now studying can be used in your parish work. Does it address the needs of any of my parishioners? How will I pass the benefit of my study on to those people?

Another way to keep study from being an escape is to keep the office door open. Resist sanctifying your study time so completely that people have to fear approaching you during that time. Don't feel ashamed about being caught with feet up and a book in your hands.

Plan a program of continuing education. Don't fake it. Don't take those extra two weeks beyond vacation for more fishing time. Sign up for something that obligates you to work at learning. Sit at the feet of an instructor again. Give away some of the control over what ideas enter your mind. Self-directed study is fine for continuous education, but it implies total control by the student. Sign up for something that allows someone else to tell you what to read and what to write.

The infusion of new ideas can resurrect a ministry on the verge of going stale.

"Without the discipline of hard study, prophecy becomes raving . . . banal . . . irrelevant."[76]

CAREER PLANNING

It is difficult to preplan a career and the course of its moves. Still, there are some signposts and directions to consider.

It is a mistake to think of any church as a stepping-stone to the next and better stage. You will treat that church like a stepchild church, as if it is not a full partner in your life. If your career plan implicitly or explicitly calls you to "endure this place" for a couple of years until you can get where the action is, then you give the church short shrift, and probably your own career too. Bad planning.

Plan to be in each parish as long as the church still seems to need your ministry and as long as you and your family feel fulfilled there. There will be more on the timing of a move in Chapter 5.

Be aware of three commonly recognized crisis points in the careers of many ministers.[77] They are (1) the first three to five years, which are a time of testing and experimentation. That's when the minister experiences several dramatic role changes, from student to pastor, learner to teacher. The career gets a shakedown cruise. There can be some severe blows. (2) Around age forty. It is a point of no return. It may be too late to have any real selectivity in alternate careers. (3) Ages sixty to sixty-five, when we begin to face retirement. There are worries about finances, health, location, and the severing of significant relationships.

I have observed another critical period for some pastors—age fifty-four. It wouldn't be true for everyone, but I know ministers who wished they had planned their careers in such a way as to make a move possible before they reached the age of fifty-four. Their experience was that at fifty-three they seemed much younger and acceptable to pastor-seeking committees than at age fifty-four.

Indeed, I have heard ministers say they found themselves most acceptable to pastor-seeking committees just before ages thirty-five, forty-five, and—for their last move—between ages forty-eight and fifty-three.

5

GETTING OUT

WHEN TO LEAVE YOUR CURRENT PARISH

How do you know when you should move? There is no set number of years.

Sometimes we move to beat the tar and feathers. Sometimes we move because we genuinely feel we have done all we can do. Sometimes it's because we have a convincing call from another church. Sometimes health conditions move us—a daughter needs to be near a large medical center. These are some of the simple, honest, and honorable things that help us to know it's time.

But take the parish into consideration. Its needs are important as well as yours. Pastors tend to stay too short a time rather than too long. Some small parishes suffer by having a parade of pastors who come and go every two or three years. All one can do in so short a time is lay foundations for good work. Therefore, those small churches are always getting foundations, but no pastor ever stays long enough to build something meaningful on those foundations.

"The most productive years for the typical pastor are years five, six, seven, and eight."[78] The most satisfying years often begin in the eighth or ninth year in a parish. The gloomiest time is often in the third year.[79] Go beyond it, and the sun may begin to shine again.

Schaller suggests thinking in terms of chapters.[80] Chapters of work, like eras. The completion of a building program would be the end of a chapter. The development of a stage of programming might be a chapter. Reaching a stage of commitment to mission might be a chapter. He then offers these clues for leaving a parish: (1) If your current chapter has run five or more years, you may consider leaving. You may be in a rut. Few "alive" chapters run more than three or four years. (2) If you cannot see a new chapter ahead of the one you are in, it's probably time to go.

MAKING THE MOVE

One minister I know used his last Sunday in the pulpit to say, "You people are the most sinful people I know, and everywhere I go I am going to tell how awful you are." There are more graceful ways to leave.

I've found that pastors who take more than a month to leave after the announcement of their departure burden the congregation with prolonged good-bys and hate-to-lose-you rituals. They also overload their own capacity to bear the lame-duck stage.

Some pastors try to leave without any farewell functions. They think it a becoming act of humility to reject going-away parties. They thereby deny congregations something they need very much—what one friend referred to as the funeral celebrations by which they naturally and lovingly set one worker aside and prepare to accept another. Don't deny the congregation its appropriate farewell ceremonies. It is a necessary function for closing a chapter in the life of a congregation. Otherwise some people will feel burdened by guilt for never seeing Pastor Johnson off properly.

Get things in good shape before you leave. Don't leave things in shambles. Make sure all records are up-to-date, that all files are current and cleaned of anything other people wouldn't need or understand. I tried to leave my desk and office extraordinarily clean. After the moving van departed, we took cleaning equipment we had kept from the movers and cleaned floors and counters in the manse we lived in. We filled every nail hole we'd placed in walls. The parish had been very good to us. We didn't want to leave a mess for them.

If your church has a good personnel committee, or your judicatory a good pastoral committee, it may ask for an exit interview. That can be a special time for honest sharing which can give good guidance for future work in the organization. Parishes can benefit from a good exit interview. If it is two-way and well done, the departing pastor can often learn some important things to guide him or her in the next parish. The exit interview is best conducted by a third party, perhaps a trusted pastor from another church. A portion of the time could well be spent interviewing the spouse too. The church might learn some important things about relating to the spouse of the pastor, or about things that need to be done in the manse.

The exit interview with the pastor could cover the evolution of the role understanding while the pastor has been in the parish, conversations about the adequacy of salary for pastoral and nonpastoral staff members, discussion about talents and skills the departing pastor thinks the next pastor might best have, and so on. It should not be an angry time but a helpful time for all parties involved.

The last thing I said from the pulpit on my last Sunday was that my pastoral work was now done in that community. I would always hold the congregation dear, but I asked them not to call on me for pastoral services. We could remain friends, but their next pastor needed to be their pastor completely. Until he or she came, I might be able to conduct a funeral when needed, assuming the schedule in my new parish would permit. But after their new pastor arrived, I would not accept any appeals to conduct the services he or she should conduct. I asked their help in respecting that policy.

I discovered one more important aspect to moving. Do not carry with you the cherished notion that all your wonderful ideas and programs can be carted off to benefit the next parish. Peter Drucker notes: "The most common cause of executive failure is inability or unwillingness to change with the demands of a new position. The executive who keeps on doing what he has done successfully before he moved is almost bound to fail."[81] Move on to new ideas and new options.

BEING A FORMER PASTOR

A pastor near me was greatly burdened by a sealed envelope he found in his desk when he arrived to begin his new work in a church. His predecessor had left this private parcel of paragraphs on almost every member of the parish. The descriptions were mostly acid ones. The former pastor had sought to help the new pastor by advising him of such things as the nasty people to stay away from. My friend was deprived of his own discoveries, except that he found that many of the people were better than their paragraphs had described them to be.

I left an envelope of the keys the pastor would need, together with a sentence wishing him or her well.

Let the parish go. Don't make yourself available to rescue the parish or to hear from friends the "terrible" things the new pastor is doing. When you are trapped, be as supportive of your successor as possible.

IN CLOSING

It is encouraging to me to be a minister and to know, as I hope you can know, that there are many people who are deeply concerned about the church of Jesus Christ, and about us; that we have the privilege of meeting people on the deepest levels of life; and that we have all those things and also the freedom to grow and flourish in our own faith.

I've talked a lot about techniques for a model for ministry which have worked well for me. But you and I must ever guard ourselves against using techniques for the sake of techniques. We utilize the best techniques like a good physician uses the best technology—to do a better job for those we serve.

Just remember that you and I have the most important job there is. If a person's heart is set to glorify the Lord with the best service mind and body can offer, there can be nothing comparable to the ministry. Let's do it well!

NOTES

1. James R. Blackwood, *The Soul of Frederick W. Robertson* (Harper & Brothers, 1947), pp. 22-23, 28.

2. Lyle E. Schaller, *Hey, That's Our Church!* (Abingdon Press, 1975), p. 46.

3. *"The Small Church in the Synod of Lakes and Prairies,"* Report to the Synod, The United Presbyterian Church U.S.A., January 1975, p. 3.

4. "Supporting an Effective Ministry," Report of the National Council of Churches, 1974, p. 13.

5. Lyle E. Schaller (in lectures in Omaha, Nebraska, July 8-14, 1976) suggests that ministers take seriously the fact that firstborn children tend to be aggressive, leading people and that middle or later-born people tend to be better team participants and followers. He suggests that two firstborns may never expect to work together well. Two middle-borns may. Or, it would often work best for the senior pastor to be a firstborn and staff members to be later-borns. Firstborn people tend to be task-oriented, whereas later-borns tend to be person-oriented and socially concerned.

6. John T. Molloy, *Dress for Success* (Warner Books, 1975), pp. 24-25, 227. (This book offers many important guidelines for attire that help the professional person accomplish his or her goals.) And John T. Molloy, on NBC-TV's *First Tuesday*, Aug. 7, 1973.

7. Lyle E. Schaller *(Hey, That's Our Church!)* has suggested some of these signs.

8. "Forum on Stewardship and Finance," *Your Church*, January/February 1976, p. 37.

9. Lyle E. Schaller, *The Decision-Makers* (Abingdon Press, 1974), p. 46.

10. Warren Bennis, *The Unconscious Conspiracy: Why Leaders Can't Lead* (AMACOM, Publishing Division of American Management Associations, 1976), pp. 172-176.

11. Donald P. Smith, *Clergy in the Cross Fire* (Westminster Press, 1973), p. 74.

12. Bennis, *Unconscious Conspiracy,* p. 173.

13. Ibid., p. 177.

14. Charles Prestwood, *The New Breed of Clergy* (Wm. B. Eerdmans Publishing Co., 1972), p. 49.

15. Ibid., p. 56.

16. Gerald J. Jud, Edgar W. Mills, and Genevieve Walters Burch, *Ex-Pastors* (Pilgrim Press, 1975), p. 41.

17. Robert Moats Miller, *How Shall They Hear Without a Preacher? The Life of Ernest Fremont Tittle* (University of North Carolina Press, 1971).

18. Jud, Mills, and Burch, *Ex-Pastors,* p. 41.

19. James D. Glasse, *Putting It Together in the Parish* (Abingdon Press, 1972), pp. 20-21.

20. "On Ministerial Expectations," *Presbyterian Outlook,* April 19, 1976, p. 11.

21. Jeffrey K. Hadden, *The Gathering Storm in the Churches* (Doubleday & Co., Doubleday Anchor Books, 1969), p. 32

22. Ibid., p. 247.

23. Interview with Dr. Patricia H. Hexum, Executive Director of the Hudson Center, 12119 Pacific Street, Omaha, Nebr.

24. John T. Molloy, on NBC-TV's *First Tuesday,* Aug. 7, 1973.

25. Carroll A. Wise, *The Meaning of Pastoral Care* (Harper & Row, 1966), p. 12.

26. "On Ministerial Expectations," p. 11.

27. A September 1974 survey conducted by the author in a small rural United Presbyterian congregation, and in suburban United, ALC Lutheran, and Christian (Disciples) congregations. Fifty-five percent of all respondents indicated "showing love." The next highest response was 30 percent for "preaching."

28. Wise, *Pastoral Care,* p. 3.

29. "On Ministerial Expectations," p. 11.

30. Ralph J. Nichols, "Listening Is a 10-Part Skill," *Nation's Business,* July 1957, p. 1.

31. Many of the suggestions come from Jack K. Fordyce and Raymond Weil, *Managing with People: A Manager's Handbook of Organization Development Methods* (Addison-Wesley Publishing Co., 1971), p. 137.

32. Ibid., p. 32.

33. "Survey on the Work of the Pastor," *Your Church* letter, March 11, 1976.

34. Dale D. McConkey, *No-Nonsense Delegation* (AMACOM, Publishing Division of American Management Associations, 1974), p. 87.

35. Correspondence (March 1976) with the survey editor of *Your Church* magazine, and his findings from a late-1975 survey on the work of the pastor; and Smith, *Clergy in the Cross Fire*, p. 79.

36. Caroline Donnelly, "How Hard Should You Work?" *Money*, April 1975, pp. 89, 90.

37. "Management," *Boardroom Reports*, Nov. 30, 1975, p. 5.

38. "How to Make the Most of Your Time," *U.S. News & World Report*, Dec. 3, 1973, p. 46.

39. Glasse, *Putting It Together in the Parish*, p. 62.

40. Report of the Presbyterian Panel, Research Unit of the Support Agency of The United Presbyterian Church U.S.A., Room 1740, 475 Riverside Drive, New York, N.Y., July 1977.

41. W. J. McCutcheon, "Protestantism Without Reformation, or Can a Church Be Great?" *The Christian Century*, Oct. 25, 1972, pp. 1063, 1064.

42. Gallup poll, as reported in the *Omaha* (Nebraska) *World Herald*, Aug. 25, 1977, p. 76.

43. Wilfred Bockelman, "The Pros and Cons of Robert Schuller," *The Christian Century*, Aug. 20-27, 1975, p. 733.

44. Gallup poll, *Omaha World Herald*, p. 76.

45. "Survey on the Work of the Pastor," *Your Church* letter, March 11, 1976.

46. "Leadership in a Small Church and Role Expectations," Synod of Lakes and Prairies, The United Presbyterian Church U.S.A., 1974.

47. John R. Brokhoff, "Will Tomorrow's Minister Preach?" *Preaching Today*, January/February 1973, p. 14.

48. Miller, *How Shall They Hear Without a Preacher?* p. 203.

49. Ibid., p. 180.

50. Ibid., p. 168.

51. Edward S. Zelley, "How to Say a Few Words," *Nation's Business*, July 1966, p. 3.

52. Rachel Conrad Wahlberg, "3,896 Sermons," *The Christian Ministry*, July 1973, pp. 16-17.

53. Zelley, "How to Say a Few Words," pp. 1-2.

54. Ibid., p. 4.

55. "Good Grief: It's Slow," *Datalert*, March 1, 1977, p. 4.

56. Dr. James R. Belt, Omaha, to wife of author, Nov. 30, 1973.

57. Schaller, *Decision-Makers,* p. 47.

58. Ibid., p. 211.

59. Authored by Robert Hale. Source unknown.

60. Presbyterian Panel, July 1977.

61. Douglas W. Johnson and George W. Cornell, *Punctured Preconceptions* (Friendship Press, 1972), p. 16.

62. James S. Stewart, *The Life and Teachings of Jesus Christ,* Vol. 2 (Edinburgh: Church of Scotland Publications Committee, 1933), p. 78.

63. "How to Make the Most of Your Time," p. 46.

64. "Forum on Stewardship and Finance," *Your Church,* January/February 1976, p. 36.

65. Smith, *Clergy in the Cross Fire,* p. 30.

66. Laile Bartlett, "Big Piece in the Jig-Saw," pp. 9-10.

67. Miller, *How Shall They Hear Without a Preacher?* p. 103.

68. Reported by the Vocation Agency of The United Presbyterian Church U.S.A., 475 Riverside Drive, New York, N.Y., Oct. 29, 1977.

69. Miller, *How Shall They Hear Without a Preacher?* p. 44.

70. Kenneth R. Mitchell, "The Tacit Contract About Money," *Monday Morning,* March 11, 1974, p. 4.

71. "Supporting an Effective Ministry," Report of the NCC, 1974, p. 13.

72. Harry Emerson Fosdick, *The Living of These Days: An Autobiography* (Harper & Brothers, 1956), p. 145.

73. Yoshio Fukuyama, "The Ministry as a Profession: Empirical Assessment," pp. 100-101.

74. Smith, *Clergy in the Cross Fire,* p. 56.

75. Lyle E. Schaller, lectures in Omaha, Nebraska, July 8-14, 1976.

76. Miller, *How Shall They Hear Without a Preacher?* p. 189

77. Glasse, *Putting It Together in the Parish,* pp. 40, 41.

78. Schaller, *Hey, That's Our Church!* p. 96.

79. Schaller lectures, Omaha, Nebraska, July 8-14, 1976.

80. Ibid.

81. Peter F. Drucker, *The Effective Executive* (Harper & Row, 1967), p. 58.

INDEX